THE RING LEGENDS OF TOLKIEN

To my aunt and uncle, Mary and Bob Maggs.

Thunder Bay Press
An imprint of Printers Row Publishing Group
9717 Pacific Heights Blvd, San Diego, CA 92121
www.thunderbaybooks.com • mail@thunderbaybooks.com

Text copyright © David Day 2020
Artwork, design and layout copyright © Octopus Publishing Group Ltd 2020

THUNDER BAY PRESS
Publisher: Peter Norton • Associate Publisher: Ana Parker
Senior Developmental Editor: April Graham
Editor: Traci Douglas

PYRAMID
Publisher: Lucy Pessell
Editor: Sarah Kennedy
Designer: Hannah Coughlin
Copy Editor: Robert Tuesley Anderson
Indexer: MFE Editorial Services
Senior Production Manager: Peter Hunt

Illustrations by Victor Ambrus (130), Jaroslav Bradac (cover, 25), Allan Curless (33, 75, 206, 226–227, 229, 231, 270), Gino D'Achille (182), Michael Foreman (34–35, 90, 202–203), David Kearney (56, 141), Pauline Martin (73), Mauro Mazzara (endpapers, 13, 38–39, 50–51, 58, 61, 67, 76–77, 97, 102–103, 113, 120, 123, 208, 242, 244, 290–291, 295), Ian Miller (68–69, 79, 107, 176, 118–119, 153, 159, 223, 238, 240, 260, 265, 277, 288), Andrew Mockett (253), Turner Mohan (43, 44, 95, 156, 165, 212, 255, 281), Kip Rasmussen (40, 104, 110, 143, 189, 125, 146, 150), Sarka Skorpikova (55, 98, 155, 201), Jamie Whyte (17, 27, 37, 114 134–135, 136, 145, 249), Robert Zigo (180, 194–195, 221, 268–269, 284, 296–297)

Library of Congress Control Number: 2020938688
ISBN: 978-1-64517-441-7

Printed in China
26 25 24 23 22   2 3 4 5 6

THE RING LEGENDS OF TOLKIEN

DAVID DAY

THUNDER BAY
P · R · E · S · S

San Diego, California

CONTENTS

———•———•———

INTRODUCTION

Tolkien once described how the discovery of the One Ring in an Orc cavern by Bilbo Baggins was as much a surprise to him as it was to his Hobbit hero, knowing, at the time, as little of its history as Bilbo Baggins did. Tolkien has previously explained how it grew from a simple vehicle of plot in *The Hobbit* into the central image of his epic tale *The Lord of the Rings*.

So just how did this incredibly important ring emerge so casually from the caverns of Tolkien's mind, with little to no indication of how significant a symbol it would become in, arguably, one of the greatest fantasy stories ever told? To more fully understand this, it is important to first consider the tradition of a type of storytelling referred to as "ring quest tales". The term is a self-explanatory one and refers to a tale or story with the symbol of the ring at its centre. Such tales are an ancient form of storytelling that are thought to date back to a time before the pyramids of Egypt were built or the walls of Babylon were raised. While the glorious civilization of Greece and the mighty empire of Rome rose and fell, the tradition of ring quest tales lived on, surviving the fall of the pagan gods, the rise of Buddha, Muhammad and Christ.

We can garner a rough idea of the early forms the ring quest took from observations made of the nomadic tribes of Lapland and Siberia in the 20th century, among whom symbolic rituals of the quest long remained intact. Anthropologists living among the shamanic Laplanders during the last century have frequently recorded the ritual enactment of the ring quest. In this ceremony the shaman or wizard of the tribe places a brass ring on the head of a sacred drum. The designs and markings on the skin of the drum are essentially a cosmic map of the human and spirit worlds. The shaman begins to chant and gently tap the rim of the drumhead with his drum hammer, making the ring move and dance. The ring's progress can be likened to the journey of the human soul, and as it moves around the cosmic map, the shaman sings the tale of the soul's perilous journey through the human and spirit worlds.

Though the bookish Oxford don who was J. R. R. Tolkien and the nomadic tribal shaman may seem worlds apart, they are intrinsically linked by the single tradition of ring quest tales that span more than five thousand years. In producing a final typescript for his publisher, Tolkien tapping on his typewriter keys set the wandering soul of his Hobbit hero on a journey that moved and danced to a pulse akin to that tapped out by the shaman on his drum. And the journey of Tolkien's One Ring across the map of Middle-earth is not so unlike the journey of the shaman's ring across the drum map of his human and spirit worlds.

It is also important to consider the significance of myth when tracing the inspiration behind Tolkien's One Ring. The richness of this heritage is evident in his tales and his vast mythological structures. Tolkien was deeply committed to the study of the ancient wisdom of the human soul as preserved in myth and legend. In *The Lord of the Rings*, he awoke something deep in human consciousness through the universal language of mythic images drawn from the early history of humankind. His extraordinary tale confirms his place as one of the greatest heirs to an ancient storytelling tradition rooted in a shared symbolic language of myth.

This was one of the most profound aspects of Tolkien's genius as an author. He combined a natural storyteller's ability and inventiveness with a scholar's capacity to draw from the deep well of myth, legend, literature and history. He breathed life into ancient traditions that, but for him, would have remained forever unknown to the large majority of modern readers.

However, it should never be mistaken that Tolkien's creative process was a mere cobbling together of ancient lore. Richer and more profound though Tolkien's writing is for the ancient tradition it draws upon, Tolkien's art is by no means mere imitation. *The Lord of the Rings* is a highly realized and originally conceived novel that has renewed, invigorated and finally reinvented the ring quest for the 20th and 21st centuries.

The Ring Legends of Tolkien is not an attempt to examine *The Lord of the Rings* page by page, image by image. Rather, it will open a broader investigation into the rich body of literature, myth and history that inspired Tolkien in the creation of his epic fantasy world. It will look at other rings and ring quests, and will discover where many elements of his epic tale were inspired and brought into existence. Just as Tolkien's Wizard Gandalf set out to discover the history of the Hobbit's ring, so too will this book search out the history and journey of Tolkien's epic One Ring.

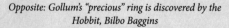

Opposite: Gollum's "precious" ring is discovered by the Hobbit, Bilbo Baggins

PART

ONE

WAR OF
THE RINGS

I n writing *The Lord of the Rings*, J. R. R. Tolkien did not invent the idea of a sorcerer-king ruling by the supernatural power of a ring. The ancient belief in the power of rings has been with the human race since the dawn of history. So much so that the quest for a ring is the basis of much of its mythology, especially in European tales. Furthermore, this belief in supernatural rings did not restrict itself to legends and fairy tales; it is very much a part of history itself.

THE ROMAN REPUBLIC

Even Tolkien's central concept of a "War of the Ring" has a remarkable historical precedent. The idea that an empire could be ruinously consumed by war because of a ring may appear an unlikely historical event, but Tolkien had no less an authority than the ancient scholar Pliny the Elder to inform him that a dispute over a ring was, in part, a cause of the downfall of the Roman Republic. Pliny wrote that a quarrel over the possession of a ring erupted between the famous demagogue Drusus and the chief senator, Caepio. The dispute led directly to a blood feud and the outbreak of the Social War (91 BCE – 88 BCE), which resulted in the collapse and ruin of the Republic of Rome.

VENICE, c.1000

Another historical tradition attributes the downfall of the once-mighty sea empire of the Republic of Venice directly to a ring. In its days of glory, Venice was the ruler of the Mediterranean by virtue of its ships. To celebrate its maritime power, the Doge of Venice would sail out into the Adriatic

THE SORCEROR OF COURTRAY'S DEMON RING

GOLD WEDDING RING OF VENICE AS BRIDE OF THE SEA

ALICE PERRERS'S MAGIC RINGS

CARVEN VIKING RING DESIGN

DACTYLIOMANCER'S RING ON A THREAD

RINGS ON THE WATER'S SURFACE IN A SERVING BOWL

EXECETUS STRIKING HIS RINGS TOGETHER

Sea with great pomp and ceremony one day each year. To celebrate Venice's "marriage" as the "bride of the sea", the Doge would throw a gold ring into the deep blue waters of the Adriatic. Several months after one such ceremony, the Doge held a state dinner at which a large fish was served at his table. When the fish was placed on the Doge's plate it was found to have the gold ring in its belly. The return of the wedding ring was widely interpreted as the sea's rejection of Venice as its bride and a premonition of disaster for the Republic. Historical events soon confirmed the prophecy. That same year marked the reversal of Venice's fortunes in its battles at sea, and the collapse of the Republic's empire swiftly followed.

GELDERLAND, 1548

In the year 1548 at Arnhem, in what was then Gelderland (now a province of the Netherlands), one of the city's most respected citizens was brought before the Chancellor and accused of sortilege, or enchantment. This man was reputed to be the region's most learned and excellent physician, and knew "the cure and remedie for all manner of griefs and diseases", according to the churchman-scholar Hegwoad. But his wisdom was not restricted to medicine. He was always "acquainted with all newes, as well forrein as domesticke".

Accusers stated that the physician obtained his powers from a ring that he wore on his hand. Witnesses claimed that the doctor – who later became known as the Sorcerer of Courtray – constantly consulted the ring. It was stated that "the ring had a demon enclosed in it, to whom it behoved him to speak every five days".

Despite the marked reluctance of the Chancellor to pass judgement on such a valued citizen, he found the evidence was so overwhelming that he had no choice but to find the man guilty. The physician was immediately proscribed for sorcery, and put to death. Curiously, even greater importance was placed on the fate of the ring than the fate of the sorcerer.

The Chancellor commanded that after the execution of the physician, the ring must be cut from his hand. So that all might witness its destruction, the ring was taken immediately to the public market. In full view of the citizens of Arnhem, the demon ring was "layd on an anvil, and, with an iron hammer beaten in pieces".

ENGLAND, 1376

In the St Albans *Chronicon Angliae*, in the year 1376, is recorded the extraordinary trial of Alice Perrers, a mistress of Edward III, King of England. Alice Perrers was a woman "neither voluptuous nor beautiful, but of smooth tongue" whom Parliament charged with having enchanted the king by use of magic rings. Through the power of these rings, it was claimed, Alice Perrers had alienated Edward's affections from his queen, involved him in illicit sexual frenzies, and held sway over his judgments in court. In the trial it was revealed that she had a master who was a magician, who was found to have effigies of Alice and the king. It was stated that the magician used herbs and incantations devised by the great Egyptian magus Nectanabus, and "used rings such as Moses used to make – rings of oblivion and memory – so that the King was unable to act any day without consulting his false predictions".

Because of the King's intervention, it proved impossible to bring down the full and fatal force of the law of the time onto the accused. However, Alice Perrers was banished from court and noble society forever after.

BYZANTIUM, 370 CE

In the year 370, during the reign of the Roman Emperor Valens, a powerful group of aristocrats feared that their monarch was neither strong nor wise enough to remain in power for long. Concerned about their own fate and that of the empire, the aristocrats secretly consulted an oracle.

The oracle practiced dactylomancy, or "ring divination". This form of prophecy was achieved by means of a circle drawn on the temple floor. The circumference of the circle was inscribed with the letters of the alphabet, and a gold ring was suspended from the temple ceiling by a long thread directly over the centre of the circle.

When the question "Who should succeed to the throne of the Emperor Valens?" was put to the oracle, the gold ring slowly but decisively drifted from letter to letter, and spelled out: "T-H-E-O-D".

All who observed the oracle believed this could only mean Theodorus, a man of noble lineage, eminent qualifications and high popularity. However, among the gathering of aristocrats was a spy loyal to Valens. When Valens learned of the oracle, he concluded that Theodorus could only come to power by means of a conspiracy. Although there was no evidence at all that Theodorus had any intention of plotting against him, the Emperor Valens had the man immediately put to death.

The great British historian Edward Gibbon remarks on the peculiar irony of this well-documented prophecy in his monumental *Decline and Fall of the Roman Empire*. For, in the year 378, the wild Visigoth tribes were in open revolt against imperial rule. The barbarian armies had crossed the Danube and threatened to march on the capital itself. The Imperial Army made a valiant and bloody stand at Adrianople, but, outnumbered and badly commanded, they were defeated by the Visigoths and the Emperor Valens was killed.

Out of the turmoil that followed the conquest, one ruthless general rose to power among the Spanish legions of the West. This man's name was T-H-E-O-D-osius. True to the prophecy of the ring, this unknown warlord seized control of the empire. He was crowned in Constantinople and became the Emperor Theodosius the Great.

THE ORIGINS OF DACTYLOMANCY

Dactylomancy has been seriously practiced throughout history. This belief in the power of rings was not a matter of literary invention; it was a part of everyday life. The example of dactylomancy illustrated in Byzantium is just one example of its practice. There are in fact several thousands more recordings of its use throughout history.

If we look at the Anglo-Saxon *Exeter Book*, compiled and written *c*.1000, we find a cryptic statement or unanswered riddle about a ring. It reads: "I heard of a bright ring interceding well before men, though tongue-less, though it cried not with loud voice in strong words. The precious thing spoke before men, though holding its peace. May men understand the mysterious saying of red gold, the magic speech." In part, the *Exeter Book* may be making reference to oracles that used rings long before the coming of Christ.

One method of allowing a ring to "speak", other than the one witnessed in Byzantium in the year 370, involved water, and, as the German Latin scholar Caspar Peucer described it, would appear to make a quite reasonable lie-detector test: "A bowl was filled with water, and a ring suspended from the finger was liberated in water, and so, according as the question was propounded, a declaration, or confirmation of its truth or otherwise, was obtained. If what was proposed was true, the ring, of its own accord, without any impulse struck the sides of the goblet a certain number of times."

The ancient Roman King Numa Pompilius evidently used this method of divination; while Execetus, the tyrant of the Phocians, used a means of divination based on sounds emitted by the striking of two large rings together. Still other practitioners of dactylomancy chose to throw rings or stones into pools of water and read the "rings" as they formed on the still surface. (This particular form of divination is not far removed from that of the prophetic images that appear in the watery rings of the "Mirror of Galadriel", which the Elf queen commands by the power of her ring, Nenya.)

So how did dactylomancy and the consulting of rings come to be regarded as a blasphemous practice that would come to face centuries of suppression? Is it possible that it ran parallel to the tradition of the symbol of the cross? And is it possible to trace it, and understand where, why and how it maintained its force and power?

A PAGAN SYMBOL: THE RING VERSUS THE CROSS

The ring was actually the primary symbol of a tradition that the Church saw as being in conflict with orthodox doctrines of Christianity. To understand this, one must look at the cult of witchcraft. In Margaret Murry's *The Witch Cult in Western Europe*, the author concludes that the so-called "cult of witchcraft" in one sense was not entirely a figment of the Church's imagination. "The only explanation of the immense number of witches who were legally tried and put to death in Western Europe is that we are dealing with a religion which was spread over the whole continent and counted its members in every rank of society, from the highest to the lowest." Murry identifies this "religion" as the remnant of primitive pagan cults which survived in various states of imperfection throughout Europe.

It is a more than reasonable supposition that aspects of pagan religions survived Christian conversion. In fact, a common tactic in the conversion of pagans was absorption of many aspects of pagan worship into the gospel of the Church. At other times, however, the Christian fathers found that if they had sufficient power it was easier to simply crush any pagan practice that was believed to pose a threat to orthodox Christian doctrines. If these surviving pagan beliefs were to be represented by any single image in the way that Christianity is represented by the cross, there is no doubt that that single image was the ring.

In Europe the ring was the dominant symbol of all the pagan Teutonic tribes. It was especially the dominant symbol of the Viking warrior culture, which was Christian Europe's greatest scourge at the end of the first millennium.

Above all others, the Vikings' one-eyed sorcerer god, Odin, was "the God of the Ring". (He was Tolkien's primary source of inspiration for his sorcerer Sauron, Lord of the Rings.) In the same way as the worship of Christ was symbolized by the cross, the worship of Odin was symbolized by the ring. After the collapse of Roman authority, European Christian settlements, churches and monasteries experienced centuries of relentless Viking terror. It is little wonder that, in the simplest terms, the Church saw in the symbol of the ring the greatest threat to the authority of the cross. It is more complex than this, of course. The ring was a much older symbol of authority than Christianity, and the Church itself adapted its authority in many forms. The Pope wore a ring as the symbol of office, as did all other officers of the Church. Christian marriages were enforced by what amounted to the pagan custom of swearing an oath upon a ring. Nuns were "wed" to Christ with a gold ring; and, in the form of the Celtic cross, the image of the ring and the cross were even united as an image suitable for worship in a Christian church.

It was a matter of where a particular ring's power was rooted. In the figure of the early Christianized Viking King Olaf, we see a real blood-and-thunder missionary who believed he knew where the source of one particular ring's power was to be found. When the Faroe Islands were converted by Olaf, the heroic Faroese chieftain Sigmundur Brestisson accepted Christianity as the new faith of his people. However, Olaf learned that Sigmundur had kept in his possession one sacred gold ring from the pagan temples. Knowing exactly the symbolic implications of Sigmundur's act, King Olaf demanded it be given up to the Church. The milder Christian virtues were not yet apparent in King Olaf. When Sigmund refused to give up the ring, Olaf had him murdered in his sleep.

RING-MAKING: THE ART OF THE SMITH

◆

The secret of the ring is in its making. To make a ring, one must have the knowledge to smelt and forge metal. The "secret language" of the smith – symbolized by the ring – was his knowledge of metallurgy. Ultimately, this is concerned with the secret of the smelting and forging of iron, which is believed to have been discovered around 1000 BCE in the region of the Caucasus Mountains. It was the atomic secret of its day, a secret that was closely guarded: where the ore was mined, how the metal was extracted, how it was forged into weapon and tools. The smith's extraordinary skill must have seemed reminiscent of the practice of alchemy in that such knowledge must have been perceived as somewhat magical or otherworldly. Because of alchemists' seemingly magical practices, they were often executed as sorcerers or magicians. The significance of alchemy is looked at more closely later on in this book.

Those who possessed the secret of the smith conquered and often exterminated those who did not. The Iron Age transformed nations of timid shepherds and farmers into ferocious warriors capable of catastrophic feats of destruction on their once-powerful, and now-subjugated, neighbours. The hero who won the smith's – or the alchemist's –"ring" in the form of the secret of iron-smelting literally saved his nation.

The arts of the smith and the occult sciences

are overlapping techniques handed down as trade secrets with their own rites and rituals. The mysteries of initiation rites and the secret language of the rituals of the trade became symbols in mythic tales.

It is not commonly recognized how profound an impact the rituals and rites of metallurgy have had on myth. However, it is not so much the techniques of metallurgy that are conveyed in these myths, but the secret rituals of initiation into those cults and the spiritual rites practiced within the guild, which evolve into the symbols of myth. The symbolic language of the ring quest, at its most profound, is concerned with the "spiritual" consequences of the Bronze and Iron Ages, which changed forever the human condition and perception of the world. Mircea Eliade emphasizes this point: "Before changing the face of the world, the Iron Age engendered a large number of rites, myths and symbols which have reverberated throughout the spiritual history of humanity."

If one looks at the ring quest myths of most cultures, there are certain constants for the hero in his pursuit of the ring: the magician, the smith, the warrior, the sword, the dwarf, the maiden, the treasure and the dragon. These all relate originally to the rites and processes of metallurgy, and later to the symbolic "secret language" of the alchemist's ring.

In *The Lord of the Rings* we have all the elements of the ring quest, and yet something wholly original in Tolkien's own War of the Ring.

THE RINGS OF POWER IN THE SECOND AND THIRD AGE

1500 *Rings of Power forged by Sauron and Elven-smiths of Eregion (Three Elf Rings, Seven Dwarf Rings, Nine Rings for Men)*

1603 *War of Sauron and Elves. Three Elf Rings hidden (Gil-galad in Lindon, Círdan in Grey Havens, Galadriel in Lothlórien)* **1600** *Sauron forges One Ring in Fires of Mount Doom*

2251 *Ringwraiths, slaves of the Nine Rings, come to serve Sauron*

3430 *Last Alliance of Elves and Men formed*

3441 *One Ring cut from Sauron's hand. Mordor falls. Sauron and Ringwraiths vanish*

1 *Gil-galad's Elf-ring goes with Elrond to Rivendell*

2 *Battle of Gladden Fields. One Ring lost in Anduin River*

1000 *Sauron in Mirkwood, secretly gathers Rings*

1050 *Wizards come to Middle-Earth. Círdan gives Elf-ring to Gandalf*

1200 *Ringwraiths appear in north*

1300 *Lord of Ringwraiths becomes Witch-king of Angmar*

1975 *Angmar destroyed*

1980 *Ringwraiths dwelling in Mordor*

2002 *Witch-king begins rule in Minas Morgul*

2470 *Gollum takes One Ring into Misty Mountains*

2463 *One Ring found by Déagol in Anduin River*

2845 *Sauron seizes last of the Seven Dwarf Rings*

2941 *Bilbo Baggins finds One Ring in the Misty Mountains*

3001 *Bilbo Baggins gives One Ring to Frodo Baggins*

3018 *Fellowship of the Ring formed*

3021 *The War of the Ring begins. One Ring destroyed. Mordor falls. Sauron and Ringwraiths vanish forever*

3021 *Keepers of the Elf Rings sail to Undying Lands*

PART

TWO.

NORSE MYTHOLOGY

No people in history were as obsessed with the power of the ring as the Vikings. The ring was wealth, honour, fame and destiny to these warrior people. Under its sign they charted unknown seas, waged barbarous wars, sacrificed man and beast, pledged their faith, made great gifts of it, and, finally, died for it. Their gods were ring lords of the heavens, and their kings were ring lords of the earth.

In the ring quest myths of the Vikings, that ferocious warrior culture of Norsemen, we see one of the primary sources of inspiration for Tolkien's fantasy epic, *The Lord of the Rings*. Although the symbol of the ring was widespread and prominent in many far more ancient cultures, it was the Norsemen who brought the ring quest to its fullest expression, and to the very heart of their cultural identity. Virtually all subsequent ring quest tales in myth and fiction are deeply indebted to the Norse myths. *The Lord of the Rings*, although striking in its originality and innovation, is no exception.

NORSE RING-GIVERS AND RING-HOARDS

Among the Vikings, the gold ring was a form of currency, a gift of honour, and sometimes an heirloom of heroes and kings. (Such a ring belongs to the Swedish royal house, the Swedish kings' ring known as Svíagríss.) At other times, when great heroes or kings fell, and it was thought none other would be worthy of the honour of the ring lord, the ring-hoard (the treasury of a nation or people, often made up of rings of gold) was buried with its master.

So, in barrow and cave, in mere and grave, upon burial ship sunk beneath the sea, the rings slept with their ring lords. Afterward, tales were told of dead men's curses and supernatural guardians. In Norse myth and in Tolkien's tales, guardians of treasures and ring-hoards take many forms: damned spirits, serpents, dragons, giants, dwarfs, barrow-wights and demon monsters.

POWER, FAME AND DESTINY

The rings of Norse mythology – like Tolkien's – were commonly magical rings forged by elves. These gold rings were tokens of both power and eternal fame. They were also symbolic of the highest power: destiny, the cycle of doom. Indeed, the Domhring, the Ring of Doom – the ring of monolithic stones that stood before the Temple of Thor – was perhaps the most dreaded symbol of the violent law of the Vikings. (In Tolkien, an identically named "Ring of Doom" stands outside the gates of Valmar, the city of the Valar.) In the centre of this ring of stones was the thunder god's pillar, the Thorstein. The histories tell us of its use. In the 9th century, the Irish king Maelgula Mac Dungail was made captive in the Viking enclave of Dublin. He was taken to the Ring of Doom and his back was broken upon the Thorstein. Of another such ring in Iceland, a scribe in the Christian 12th century wrote that bloodstains could still be seen upon the central stone.

Yet the great pillared temple of the fierce, red-bearded thunder god housed another very different – but to Norse society infinitely more important – ring. Thor's weapon was the hammer called Mjölnir, "Destroyer", but Thor's most valued gift to humankind was the altar ring that was housed in his temple. This was the Oath Ring of Thor, the emblem of good faith and fair dealing.

On the sacred altar was a silver bowl, an anointing twig, and the Oath Ring itself. Whether of gold or silver, it had to weigh more than 20 ounces. Thor's statue, mounted in his goat-drawn chariot, dominated the sanctuary while around the altar were grouped the 12 figures of his fellow gods, their eyes fixed upon the ring.

When an oath was to be taken, an ox was brought in and slaughtered, and the *hlaut*, the sacred blood, was sprinkled on the ring. Then the man laid his hand upon the ring and, with Thor gazing down on him, faced the people and said aloud: "I am swearing an oath upon the Ring, a sacred oath; so help me Freyr, and Njörthr and Thor the Almighty…"

For the Vikings, such an oath was legally binding, and when the world's first democratic parliament, the Althing, was established in Iceland in 930, the temple priests brought out the Oath Rings to reinforce its law.

Yet Thor was not the only ring lord among the gods, nor was the power of his ring supreme. The greatest power was in the ring on the hand of Odin, the magician and king of the gods. Odin was the Allfather, Lord of Victories, Wisdom, Poetry, Love and Sorcery. He was Master of the Nine Worlds of the Norse universe, and through the magical power of his ring he was, quite literally, "The Lord of the Rings".

But Odin was not always almighty, and his quests for power and for his magical ring were long and achieved at great cost. He travelled throughout the Nine Worlds on his quests and hid himself in many forms, but most often he appeared as an old man: a bearded wanderer with one eye. He wore a grey or blue cloak and a traveller's broad-brimmed slouch hat. He carried only a staff and was the model for the wandering wizard and magicians from Merlin to Gandalf.

NORSE COSMOLOGY AND TOLKIEN

Before delving more fully into the myth of Odin's ring, it is important to first take a look at an overview of Tolkien's cosmology and compare it to that of Norse mythology. Although Tolkien's world is profoundly different in many of its basic moral and philosophical perspectives from that of Viking mythology, similarities are numerous and significant.

The most immediate parallel for anyone even mildly familiar with Norse myth is that the world of mortal men in both Norse myth and Tolkien's world have the same name: the Norse "Midgard" literally translates to "Middle-earth".

The immortal gods of the Norsemen are made up of two races: the Æsir and the Vanir, while Tolkien's "gods" (we should properly call them entities or spirits) are originally called the Ainur, but become known as the Valar in their earthly form. In both systems, the gods live in great halls or palaces in a world apart from mortal lands. The Æsir live in Asgard, which can be reached only by crossing the Rainbow Bridge on the flying horses of the Valkyries. Tolkien's Valar live in Aman, which, after the reshaping of Arda at the end of the Second Age, can be reached only by crossing the "Straight Road" in the flying ships of the Elves.

Next page: Mahanaxar the "Ring of Doom" – the sacred circle of standing stones before the gates of Valmar, the city of the Valarian "gods" of Arda

NINE WORLDS

———◆———

Norse cosmology was rather more complex than Tolkien's in its elemental structure. Asgard and Midgard were just two of its nine "worlds". However, Tolkien's "worlds" are far more cosmopolitan and most of the inhabitants of the nine Norse worlds are recognizable within his two.

Besides the worlds of Midgard and Asgard, Norse myths tell of the worlds called Alfheim and Swartalfheim: the realms of the light elves and the dark elves. These were parallel to Tolkien's Elves, who are divided into two great races: the Eldar, who are (for the most part) Light Elves, and the Avari, who are Dark Elves.

The dwarfs of Viking mythology were also given their own world. This was a dark underground world of caves and caverns called Nidavellir, which was found beneath Midgard, where the dwarfs constantly worked their mines. These dwarfs share many of the characteristics of Tolkien's Dwarves, although in Tolkien both Dwarves and Elves are more highly defined and individual, and their genealogies are far more complex.

It is notable that Tolkien took the names of most of his Dwarves directly from the text of Iceland's 12th-century *Prose Edda*. The *Edda* gives an account of the creation of the dwarfs, then lists their names. All the Dwarves in *The Hobbit* appear on this list: Thorin, Dwalin, Balin, Kíli, Fíli, Bifur, Bofur, Bombur, Dori, Nori, Ori, Óin and Glóin. Other names of Dwarfs which Tolkien found in the *Prose Edda* included Thráin, Thror, Dáin and Náin. The *Edda* also gives the name Durin to a mysterious creator of the dwarfs, which Tolkien uses for his first Dwarf king of "Durin's Line".

Next spread: The swan ships of the Elves sailing from the world of mortal Men over the "Straight Road" to Eldamar

Rather surprisingly, another of the Icelandic dwarfs is named Gandalf. Undoubtedly, however, it was the literal meaning of Gandalf – "sorcerer elf" – that appealed to Tolkien when choosing this name for his Wizard.

The Norsemen gave two worlds to their races of giants: Jötunheim and Muspelheim. Jötunheim was the home of the cave-dwelling rock and frost giants. In them we see the recognizable characteristics of the large, stupid and easily outwitted monsters that evolved into the trolls of Scandinavian fairy tales. In Tolkien, these became his similarly stupid Stone Trolls and Snow Trolls.

In the world of Muspelheim, however, we find the far more formidable fire giants. Undoubtedly fire giants are personifications of volcanic subterranean powers. For once released from Muspelheim, fire giants were virtually unstoppable. In Ragnarök, the final battle of gods and giants at the end of time, they played a major part in the destruction of the world. In Tolkien, we see something of these terrible titans in his creation of the Balrogs, the fiery "demons of might".

Another world was Vanaheim, the home of the second race of gods, the Vanir, a race of nature spirits of the earth and air who are also magicians capable of casting terrifying spells. In Norse myth these magician gods are not clearly defined as the dominant Æsir gods, but they seem to resemble Tolkien's Valar in their early manifestations as elemental spirits or "forces of nature".

The deepest world of all was Niflheim, the dark and misty land of the dead. In this cold and poisoned land was the great walled citadel of Hel, the goddess of the dead. The gate of the fortress of Hel was guarded by Garm the Hound, and within were imprisoned the damned spirits of the dead. This is

Opposite: First of the Seven Fathers of the Dwarves –
King Durin the Deathless

comparable in Tolkien's *Silmarillion* to the cold and poisoned land of Angband ("iron fortress"), which is ruled by Morgoth, the spirit of darkness. The gate of the fortress of Angband was guarded by Carcharoth the Wolf, and within were imprisoned many Elves who were hideously tortured and transformed into a race of damned beings called Orcs. By the time of the War of the Ring, Morgoth's disciple Sauron attempts to recreate Angband in his dark and evil land of Mordor.

THE FINAL BATTLE

Ultimately, Norse myth and Tolkien's fiction both had cosmologies that share a stoic fatalism in their ultimate destiny. In Viking myth, the spirits of slain warriors are gathered in the Hall of Valhalla in Asgard, while, in Tolkien's tales, the spirits of slain Elves inhabit the Halls of Mandos in Aman. Both remain there and await the time when they are called to participate in the cataclysms that will end their worlds. This is the great conflict of elemental forces that the Vikings called Ragnarök and Tolkien called the World's End.

Tolkien's vision of his World's End is deliberately veiled, but we see some comparisons between the Viking Ragnarök – when the rebel god Loki led the giants into battle against the gods – and Tolkien's cataclysmic Great Battle in *The Silmarillion*. When Eönwë, the Herald of the Valar, blows his trumpet, the Valar go into battle against the rebel Vala Morgoth and his monstrous servants at the end of the First Age of Sun. The Viking Ragnarök was a battle between the gods and the Giants, which similarly commenced when Heimdall, the Herald of the Gods, blew his horn. Ragnarök ended with the destruction of all the Nine Worlds. Tolkien's

Opposite: Norse Gods in contention with the Giants and monstrous elemental forces for domination over the Nine Worlds

Great Battle results in the total destruction of Morgoth and his evil kingdom of Angband, but it also tragically causes the beautiful Elvish realms of Beleriand to sink beneath the sea.

Some tales in Tolkien's writing directly echo episodes in that cataclysm of Ragnarök. In the Quest of the Silmaril, the hero Beren attempts to use the fiery Silmaril to drive back Carcharoth, the Giant Wolf of Angband. However, the beast bites off Beren's hand at the wrist and swallows both hand and the flaming jewel. Carcharoth, the Red Maw, is filled with horrific pain as the jewel sears his accursed flesh and consumes his evil soul from within. The great beast is like a raging meteor loose in the land, full of pain and wrathful power until at last he is slain.

In Tolkien's tale, Carcharoth is comparable to the Norse myth of Fenrir, the Giant Wolf who bit off the hand of Tyr,

Battle of the great wolf Carcharoth and Beren
Erchamion at the Gates of Angband

the heroic son of Odin. Fenrir was the monstrous offspring of the evil rebel god Loki and, like Carcharoth, was the largest and most powerful wolf in the spheres of the world. During Ragnarök, Fenrir devoured the sun, which burned and consumed him from within but filled him with wrathful power until at last he was slain.

DESTRUCTION AND RENEWAL

In *The Lord of the Rings*, Gandalf's battle with the Balrog of Moria mirrors another duel in Ragnarök. In the giant Balrog of Moria, who fights the Wizard Gandalf with a sword of flame on the stone bridge of Khazad-dûm, we have a diminished version of Surt, the fire giant, who fights the god Freyr with a sword of flame on the Rainbow Bridge of Bifrost. Both duels end in disaster when the bridges collapse beneath them, and both the combatants hurtle down in a rage of flame.

Although both Tolkien and the Norsemen share a cataclysmic vision of the end of their cosmologies, this vision is not without hope. Out of these conflicts, both promise that this ending is also a transition: a newer, better and more peaceful world is to be reborn from the violent old one.

Tolkien's inspiration is drawn from a far wider range of sources than this brief comparison of cosmologies suggests. However, the influence of Norse myth in the shaping of Tolkien's world is undeniable. This becomes even more evident when we examine ring myths of that civilization, and especially those myths that relate to the king of the Viking gods, Odin.

PART

THREE

GOD OF
THE RING

Odin was the supreme god of the Viking culture. He was a god, poet, sorcerer, warrior, trickster, transformer, necromancer, mystic, shaman and king. Odin is also the single most important figure in any nation's mythology as a source of inspiration for Tolkien in his creation of *The Lord of the Rings*. In Odin's character we can see both of Tolkien's great magicians: Gandalf the Grey and Sauron the Ring Lord. In Odin we find one of the most complex and ambivalent figures in mythology. He is like a force of nature that is totally uninhibited by moral notions of good and evil. In his actions and deeds, he is not concerned with the morals of humans, but with the acquisition and use of power.

GOOD AND EVIL

This is a fundamental difference between the Norse Midgard and Tolkien's Middle-earth. The Norse mythic world is essentially amoral, while Tolkien's world is consumed by the great struggle between the forces of good and evil. Consequently, the attributes of the Norse world's greatest wizard, Odin, are necessarily split in two in Tolkien's morality tale: the "good" aspects of Odin are found in the Wizard Gandalf, and the "bad" aspects are found in the Necromancer Sauron.

The entire epic tale of *The Lord of the Rings* is primarily about the struggle for control of the world by these conflicting powers as embodied in this duel between the Wizard and Necromancer. And Tolkien's single great message – entirely inexplicable to the philosophy and aspirations of the Norsemen – is that "power corrupts". Tolkien's ring quest tale is about the corruption implicit in a quest for pure power, and how the pursuit of power is in itself evil. We soon learn that even when that power (as embodied in the ultimate power of the One Ring) is pursued for reasons that appear essentially "good" it will necessarily corrupt the quester. We see this in Saruman, who was originally a "good" Wizard but who demonstrates the classic moral error of believing that "the end justifies the means". In his attempt to overthrow the forces of the "evil" Sauron, Saruman gathers forces that in themselves are just as evil, and is himself corrupted by this desire for power. Unwittingly, Saruman becomes a mirror image and ally of the evil being he initially wished to overcome.

In the "good" Wizard Gandalf, we see his wisdom and strength of will in his refusal to take possession of the One Ring for a single moment, for fear of his own corruption. He knows full well that he would be morally destroyed by it, as surely as was Saruman.

WANDERING THE NINE WORLDS

In the myths of the Norsemen, all these particular dilemmas did not exist. These morally conflicting aspects are all embodied in the single figure of Odin the Wizard in his quest for dominion over the Nine Worlds. We see the lonely figure of Odin the Traveller, who had nothing but his wits to acquire the power he desired. In his wandering years, we see that his life ultimately was a ring quest for his own "One Ring". This was the magical ring called Draupnir, whose acquisition was a proclamation to all that Odin had become the "Ring Lord of the Nine Worlds".

Although the worlds of the Norsemen were not complicated by Tolkien's moral scruples, they were nevertheless aware that

Next page: Inspired by Odin – Middle-earth's greatest
magicians: Gandalf the Grey and Sauron the Ring Lord

such quests exacted a price. Odin the wanderer was a seeker of knowledge and visions. He travelled the Nine Worlds, asking questions of every living thing: giants, elves, dwarfs and spirits of the air, water, earth and woods. He questioned the trees, plants and the very stones themselves. Odin often endured many trials and dangerous adventures, but from each he wrung what wisdom there was from all things he encountered.

As Odin wandered unnoticed about Midgard – in much the manner as Tolkien's Istari, or Wizards (who in origin were Maiar, lesser spirits who served the Valar), wandered Middle-earth – his wisdom and power increased. Like Radagast the Brown, Odin learned the languages of the birds and beasts. Like Saruman the White, he acquired the honeyed tongue of poets and orators. Like Sauron the Ring Lord, he acquired mastery over wolves and ravens (or crows, in Sauron's case). Like Gandalf the Grey, Odin acquired a magical horse which could outrun the storming winds.

YGGDRASIL

In Norse myth, Yggdrasil, the great ash tree, possesses mighty limbs that encompass the Nine Worlds. Yggdrasil's top is in the heavens above Asgard, and its roots are beneath Hel. Beyond its purpose as a pillar to support these worlds, Yggdrasil is the means by which Odin makes the journey between them. Thus, we seem to have the reason for the name Yggdrasil, which literally means "the steed of Ygg [Odin]". In many respects, Odin is the "supreme shaman". For just as the shaman climbs or rides up his tree in his trance, so Odin rides Yggdrasil to the Nine Worlds.

It was on Yggdrasil that Odin underwent his most harrowing rite of passage. Similarly to the crucified Christ, Odin was wounded by a spear and hung from the sacred tree for nine days and nine nights. Hanging from the tree in great pain, Odin maintained a state of meditation on the markings cut in the stone by Yggdrasil's roots. By the ninth night Odin deciphered the marking and discovered the secret of the magical alphabet known as runes.

By the power of the runes his own resurrection was achieved. From Yggdrasil he cut the limb he was hung from and made his magician's staff. By the magic of runes Odin could cure, make the dead speak, render weapons powerless, gain women's love, and calm storms by land and sea.

Then, ever thirsting for more knowledge, Odin went to drink from the Fountain of Wisdom at Yggdrasil's foot, but for this too there was a price. For one deep draught from the fountain, Odin had to sacrifice an eye. Without hesitation he drank, and from that time he was always the one-eyed god.

In *The Lord of the Rings*, we see something of Odin's rites of passage in Gandalf the Grey's seemingly fatal battle with the Balrog. This conflict and a subsequent mystic inner journey, not unlike Odin's, eventually results in the resurrection of a "supercharged" Gandalf the White. Gandalf, who already knew how to read runes, rapidly demonstrates many new powers, the least being the ability to render weapons powerless.

With the evil Sauron, we see a Necromancer insanely obsessed with the acquisition of power. Odin becomes the one-eyed lord because he sacrifices the other eye in his quest. Sauron becomes the one-eyed lord because he sacrifices everything but that one evil eye. Nothing remains of his spirit and soul but that one fiery evil eye.

In Norse myth, this last inward journey of Odin on Yggdrasil was his making as the Magician–King. Odin ascended to Asgard, where the other gods saw his might and wisdom, and all acknowledged them. Similarly, in Tolkien, all the "Free Peoples" of Middle-earth recognized the might and wisdom of the resurrected Gandalf; and the forces of darkness recognized and accepted the dominion of Sauron in his final resurrection as the "Eye".

In his resurrected form, Odin was a fearful god to look on. He was stern, one-eyed, grey-bearded and of gigantic size. He wore a grey cloak with a broad blue mantle and a warrior's eagle-winged helmet. At his feet crouched the two fierce wolves of war ("Ravener" and "Greed"), and on one shoulder perched his two raven messenger-spies ("Thought" and "Memory"). Tolkien's king of the Valar, Manwë the Lord of the Air, is rather more in the style of the Olympian Zeus; however, he does share some of Odin's characteristics. He is stern, grey-bearded, of gigantic size, and wears a blue-mantled cloak. He is also the god of poetry, and the wisest and most powerful of gods.

THE HALLS OF ODIN

As the king of the gods, Odin possessed three great halls in Asgard. The first was Valaskiaff, where he sat on his golden throne called Hlidskialf. From here Odin's one eye could see all that happened in all the Nine Worlds.

In Tolkien's world there are three variations on Odin's throne. Manwë, the king of the Valar, is enthroned on Taniquetil, the highest mountain in the world, and his all-seeing eyes can see over all the world. Sauron's One Eye

Opposite: Taniquetil, the highest mountain in Tolkien's world of Arda

has similar, if somewhat more limited, power in its ability to see and command his domain from the Dark Tower of Mordor. And Frodo Baggins, the Hobbit, discovers the "Seat of Seeing" on Amon Hen, "the hill of the eye". Once he sits on its stone throne, like a little Odin, he can see telescopically for hundreds of miles in all directions.

Odin's second hall was called Gladsheim. This was the Council Hall of the Gods, where Odin presided over the throne ring of the 12 other gods. This is comparable to the Ring of Doom, or Council of the Valar, presided over by Manwë, at the gates of Valmar in the Undying Lands of Aman.

Most famous of all of Odin's halls was Valhalla, the "hall of the slain", the golden hall of warriors. This is the great feasting-hall with 540 doors and a roof fashioned from shields of polished gold, presided over by Odin, Lord of Victories. Here warriors who fall in battle are rewarded for their bravery by unending feasting and drinking. And there they remain

Winged Valkyrie battle maidens carrying slain heroes to Valhalla

until the time of Ragnarök. In Tolkien we have the rather more gloomy Hall of Awaiting in the Mansions of Mandos, the Speaker of Doom, in the Undying Lands. However, in common with the Viking warriors, the spirits of slain Elves await the call for the final cataclysm of the World's End.

As emblems of office, Odin was presented with two great gifts. Odin's magician's staff was taken to Alfheim, where the elf-smith Dwalin forged the head of the spear, Gungnir, the most fearful weapon of the Lord of Victories. In Tolkien an echo of this weapon is seen in the magical spear Aeglos, the most dreaded weapon of Gil-galad, the last high king of the Elves of Middle-earth.

DRAUPNIR

———◇———

However, the supreme gift, and the ultimate manifestation of the wealth and power of the Magician–King, was the ring called Draupnir. In Tolkien's tale, all the skill of the Elf Celebrimbor, the most wondrous smith of Middle-earth, and all the wisdom of Sauron, went into the forging of the Rings of Power. In Norse myth all the skill of the dwarfs Sindri and Brokk, the greatest smiths in the Nine Worlds, and all the wisdom of Odin were invested in the forging of the ring Draupnir.

Draupnir means "the dripper", for this magical golden ring had the power to drip eight other rings of equal size every nine days. Its possession by Odin was not only emblematic of his dominion of the Nine Worlds but consolidated his accumulated powers by giving him a source of almost infinite wealth. Draupnir gave Odin, in his capacity as the king of the gods, the greatest ring-hoard and allowed him to become the greatest ring-giver in the Nine Worlds.

With the acquisition of Draupnir, Odin's quest for dominion was completed. It can be no accident that Draupnir spawns eight other rings of equal weight in nine days. Through Draupnir, Odin rules Asgard, while the other eight are used by Odin the Ring Lord as gifts of wealth and power by which the other eight worlds are governed. Like the earthly Viking king who as a "ring-giver" rewards his jarls (earls), so Odin maintains the order of the other eight worlds by his gift of rings to chosen heroes and kings. The ring on his hand is the ultimate source of all magical rings and all wealth. Through his control of Draupnir, Odin literally becomes the "Lord of the Rings".

Among the many legends of Odin, one above all others deals with the ring Draupnir. This is the legend concerning the death of Odin's favourite son, Balder. After his slaying, his corpse was placed in the huge funeral ship called Ringhorn and all the gods gathered to pay homage. Each laid a gift of unspeakable wonder in his ship. However, so great was Odin's grief that, in a frenzy of despair, he placed Draupnir on his son's breast just as the ship was set alight and entirely consumed in flames.

This was a tragic error, for without the ring Odin's mastery of the Nine Worlds was in danger of being challenged by the giants. The ring was needed to restore order to the Nine Worlds. Fortunately, the ring did not perish in the funeral flames, but went with the spirit of Balder into the dark realm of Hel, the prison of the dead.

Opposite: Gilgalad, Last High King of the Noldor with Aeglos, the spear before which "none could stand"

THE QUEST FOR THE RING

So a journey has to be made down the "cosmic tree", Yggdrasil, to recover the ring. To achieve this quest, Odin mounts his magical eight-legged steed, Sleipnir, and rides down into the deepest realm of Hel. Once there, Sleipnir leaps over the chained Hound of Hel and the great gate it guards as well. Both rider and steed enter into the domain of the damned, seize the sacred ring and ride back. Once Draupnir is restored to Odin in Asgard, peace and order are restored to the Nine Worlds.

In Tolkien's *The Lord of the Rings* we have exactly the opposite scenario in Sauron the Ring Lord's evil quest to recover his One Ring. Sauron is master of a domain of the damned – the hell-on-earth called Mordor – when the One Ring is taken from him. The Ring should then have been consumed by the flames of Mount Doom, but instead it is taken out of the kingdom of the damned into the mortal world, where it is lost. Once Sauron returns to Mordor, he sends his Dark Riders into the living world in an attempt to recover the One Ring. It is obvious that, if his ring quest is achieved and the One Ring is restored to Sauron in Mordor, the result will be exactly the opposite of Odin's tale. Chaos and war would certainly consume and destroy all of the world.

*Opposite: Bilbo Baggins on the Seat of Seeing on
Amon Hen, the "Hill of the Eye"*

PART

FOUR

THE
VÖLSUNGA
SAGA

The most famous ring legend of the Norsemen is told in the *Völsunga Saga*. The epic tale is one of the greatest literary works to survive the Viking civilization. Within the *Völsunga Saga* is the history of many of the heroes of the Völsung and Nibelung dynasties. In earliest recorded sagas, the Nibelungs were called the Guikings. However, the names appear to be used interchangeably. Iceland's Snorri Sturluson, in the 13th-century *Younger Edda*, states: "Gunnar and Hogni were called Nibelungen or Guikings; therefore the gold is called the Nibelungen hoard." To minimalize the confusion in view of later Germanic traditions, I will use the Nibelung name for the dynasty.

The fates of the Völsung and Nibelung dynasties were bound up with that of a magical ring called Andvarinaut. This was the magical ring that once belonged to Andvari the Dwarf. It seems to have been an earthly Draupnir. Its name means "Andvari's loom" because it "wove" its owner a fortune in gold, and with that wealth went power and fame. The tale of Andvarinaut has become the archetypal ring legend, and is primarily concerned with the life and death of the greatest of all Norse heroes, Sigurd the Dragonslayer.

In this chapter, the *Völsunga Saga* is retold. It should be noted that the epic is a collection of over 40 linked but individual saga tales. These were the final outcome of an oral tradition of diverse authorship composed over many centuries. The resulting texts therefore often result in a somewhat irregular plot structure, although the overall outline is clear. In this retelling, those parts of the saga concerning the ring are emphasized in detail, while peripheral adventures (particularly those that precede the appearance of Sigurd) are told in synopsis form.

Readers will find many parallels between the *Völsunga Saga* and Tolkien's *The Lord of the Rings* and *The Silmarillion*. Rather than break up the tale with interjections, these parallels will be examined later, along with comparisons with the legends of King Arthur, Charlemagne, Dietrich von Berne, and numerous other heroes and traditions, including the medieval German epic *Nibelungenlied* and a score of fairy tales.

THE VÖLSUNGS

The *Völsunga Saga* begins with the tale of the hero Sigi, who is the mortal son of Odin. He is a great warrior who by his strength and skill becomes the King of the Huns. King Sigi's son is Reric, who is also a mighty warrior, but cannot give his queen a child and heir. So the gods send to Reric a crow with an apple in its beak. Reric gives this apple to his wife, who eats it and becomes heavy with child. But the child remains in his mother's womb for six years before he is released by the midwife's knife. This child is Völsung, who becomes the third in this line of kings.

Völsung is the strongest and most powerful of all the kings of Hunland. He is a man of huge physical size and he sires ten sons and one daughter. The eldest of his children are the twin brother and sister, Sigmund and Signy.

One day a grey-bearded stranger with one eye appears in the great hall of the Völsungs in the midst of a great gathering of Huns, Goths and Vikings. Without a word, the old man strides over to Branstock, the great living oak tree that stands in the centre of the Völsung hall. He draws a brilliant sword from a sheath and drives it up to its hilt in the tree trunk. The ancient stranger then walks out of the hall and disappears.

No mortal man could have achieved such a feat, and all know that this old man can be none other than Odin. All the heroes in the great hall desire this sword, but only Sigmund has the strength to draw it from Branstock. All know that, armed with Odin's sword, Sigmund is the god's chosen warrior.

With this sword, which can cut stone and steel, Sigmund wins great fame, yet terrible tragedy soon befalls the Völsung family. Sigmund's sister, Signy, is married to the King of Gothland, who treacherously murders King Völsung at the wedding feast. He then imprisons Völsung's ten sons by placing them in stocks in a clearing in the wild wood. One son is torn to pieces each night for nine nights by a werewolf, who is actually the witch-mother of the king. However, on the tenth night, Sigmund (with the help of his sister Signy) manages to trick the werewolf and slays her by tearing out her tongue with his teeth.

SIGMUND AND SIGNY

Sigmund escapes and lives for many years as an outlaw in an underground house in the wild wood. Signy's desire for vengeance for her father and brothers is great, even though she remains the wife of the King of Gothland. She casts a spell on Sigmund and goes to his underground house. Sigmund does not know it is his own sister and makes love to her. Months later, Signy has a child from this incestuous union. He is named Sinfjötli, and when he is grown, Signy

Opposite: Sigmund the Völsung drawing the sword of Odin from Branstock

sends him to Sigmund in the wild wood, so together they may avenge Völsung's death.

After many trials, including stealing and wearing werewolf skins and being buried alive in a barrow grave, Sigmund and Sinfjötli set fire to the great hall of the Goth king. Signy secretly returns Odin's sword to Sigmund, and all who attempt to escape the fire are slain. Seeing the Goth king and his kin slain, Signy confesses the price she has paid to exact her revenge, including incest with her brother, and leaps into the flames.

Sigmund returns with Sinfjötli to his homeland and claims his father's throne as King of Hunland. He rules successfully for many years, although his son Sinfjötli dies by poisoning. Shortly after King Sigmund marries the Princess Hjordis, two armies of Vikings ambush Sigmund. However, they fail to slay him

because of his supernatural sword. Into the fray of battle comes an ancient, one-eyed warrior. When Sigmund strikes this old man's spear shaft with his sword, the blade shatters. Sigmund knows his doom has come. The ancient warrior can be none other than Odin. Sigmund's enemies strike him down.

Sigmund is given mortal wounds by his enemies, yet he does not despair for he has lived long and he knows that his queen is heavy with child. The dying Sigmund tells his wife she must take the shards of Odin's sword. For Sigmund knows the prophecy that he will sire a son who, with the sword re-forged, will win a prize greater than that of any mortal man.

Sigmund's queen flees the battleground and after a long journey finds refuge in the Viking court of the King of the Sea Danes. There, the exiled queen gives birth to her son, Sigurd, and raises him in secret under the protection of the Danes.

THE APPRENTICESHIP OF SIGURD

In the realm of the Sea Danes is a master smith. He is called Regin, and from his long, toiling hours at the forge, his powerful body is hunched and stunted like a dwarf's. Yet from his fire and forge comes much beauty in jewels and bright weapons. Swords, spears and axes shine with a bright sheen. None know their equal.

No one knows Regin's age or his past. He entered the land of the Danes before the memory of the oldest king. He is no lord of fighting men, but a smith and a master of other crafts as well. He is filled with the wisdom of runes, chess play, and the languages of many lands.

But Regin casts a cold eye on life, and none knows him as a friend. So the king of the Sea Danes is much surprised when Regin fosters Sigurd and becomes his tutor. There never was a pupil like Sigurd, so quick and eager to learn. He is well taught by the smith in many arts and disciplines, although in the warrior's skills he excels most. Teacher and pupil are a strange pair. Some say Regin is too cold tempered, and Sigurd born too hot. Whatever the reason, over the years of learning, master and apprentice never form a bond of love or close friendship.

Wise though Sigurd becomes with Regin's teaching, there is something in his blood that beckons him to learn matters that are even beyond the smith's teachings. So Sigurd often goes to the forest for many days of wandering. On one such solitary journey, Sigurd meets an ancient man in a cape and a wide-brimmed slouch hat. The old man's bearded face has but one eye, and he uses a spear as a walking stick. This man tells Sigurd he may choose whatever horse he wishes for himself from his herd in the meadow.

When Sigurd chooses a young, grey stallion, the old man smiles.

"Well chosen. He is called Grani, meaning "grey-coat", and he is as sleek as quicksilver and will grow to become the strongest and swiftest stallion ever to be ridden by a mortal man. For Grani's sire was the immortal Sleipnir, the eight-legged stallion of Asgard, who rides storm clouds over the world."

Not long afterward, Regin sends for the youth.

"You have grown large and strong, Sigurd. Now is the time for an adventure," says Regin. "I have a tale to tell."

The two then go out onto the green grass before Regin's hall. By an oak tree there is a stone bench on which the smith settles, while the huge youth sits on the grass at his feet.

REGIN'S TALE

"Know me now, young Sigurd, for what I am. Not a man, but one born in a time before the first man entered the spheres of the world. This was a time almost before there was Time. Giants and dwarfs were filled with terrible strength, and there were magicians of such power that even the gods feared to walk alone across the lands of Midgard.

"In this time, the gods Odin, Hœnir and Loki went on an adventure into Midgard and dared to enter the land of my father, Hreidmar, the greatest magician of the Nine Worlds. On the first day, the three gods came to a stream and a deep pool. Resting a while, they soon saw a lithe, brown otter swimming in the pool. Diving deep, the otter caught a silver salmon in its jaws and, reaching the far shore, struggled to drag his prize out of the water. It seemed an opportunity not to be missed. Without a word, Loki hurled a stone and broke the otter's skull.

"Loki rejoiced at having won both otter and salmon

with a single stone. He went to the otter and skinned it. Taking up their double prize of salmon and otter skin, the three gods walked on until evening, when they came to a great hall upon a fair heath. This was Hreidmar the Magician's hall, which stood on the Glittering Heath just above the dark forest called the Mirkwood.

"When the three gods entered the hall, they made a gift of the salmon and the otter skin to their host. Rather than glady accepting the gifts, the magician immediately flew into a rage and bound the gods at once with a deadly spell. Then he called to me, to bring my fire-forged chains of unbreakable iron; and he called to my brother, the mighty Fáfnir, to bind these gods tightly with my chains and his pitiless strength. Once this was done, no one but the magician-king might ever free those three gods.

"Although my father much admired my craft and Fáfnir's strength, it was his third son that he loved best. This son was the magician's eyes and ears. He was a shapeshifter who travelled often in many forms of bird and beast, and told my father what went on in the wide world. He was called Ótr (Otter) after his favourite guise.

"This was the reason for the magician-king's terrible wrath. The otter that the gods slew at the pool, then unknowingly offered as a gift, was the flayed skin of their host's favourite son.

"For this outrage, the magician was intent on the destruction of all three who slew his son. But Odin spoke persuasively, saying truthfully that Ótr was slain in ignorance, and that in such cases, payment of weregild instead of blood was just and honourable compensation. Though much grieved, the magician-king laid the terms.

Mirkwood, the dark and haunted forest of Midgard

"'Fill my son's skin with gold and cover him with it too. Do that and I will spare you,' he demanded, grimly.

"Since Loki had cast the fatal stone, he was chosen to find the weregild, while the others remained bound. Odin advised him to quickly find the dwarf Andvari, who was renowned for his wealth. This hoard of gold he hid in a mountain cavern beneath a waterfall. Yet Odin warned that Andvari the dwarf was also a shapeshifter who hid his identity. Most often, he took the form of a great pike who lived in the pool beneath the falls, so he might better guard his watery treasury door.

"Loki was not long in finding the waterfall. He stared hard into the dear pool and saw the great pike hiding in the eddies under the rocks. He dragged the pike to the land where, gasping, it took on Andvari's true shape and begged for mercy. Loki was not gentle. He twisted the dwarf until his screams drowned out the sound of the water. Finally, Andvari gave up his golden treasure to Loki, but the dwarf begged that he might be allowed to keep just one red-gold ring for himself. Guessing at the ring's importance, Loki snatched the ring from Andvari as well, and hurried on his way.

"Now this was the ring called Andvarinaut, which means 'Andvari's loom', for by its power gold comes, and treasure increases ever more. This golden ring breeds gold, though this was but one of its powers; many of its other powers are unknown. This one small red-gold ring that Loki stole was worth all the rest of treasure together.

"The dwarf screamed after him: 'I curse you for this! The ring and the treasure it spawned will carry my curse forever. All who possess the ring and its treasure for long will be destroyed!'

"Loki returned to the magician's hall with the gold hoard and stuffed Ótr's skin tight with it, and piled gold over all. The price in weregild seemed to have been made, but the magician-king looked keenly at the treasure and pointed to one whisker that still protruded. Loki smiled grimly then and let fall the ring Andvarinaut which he had held back. The ring covered the last hair and the payment was made.

"The magician-king packed up the treasure in great oak chests, but took the ring Andvarinaut and placed it on his hand. Then he released the bonds of his spell, commanded Fáfnir and I to unlock the chains, and the gods were given safe passage out of his land.

"For a short time, all seemed well, but the mere sight of the ring was a torment to Fáfnir. And so, one night Fáfnir crept to our father's bed and cut his throat while he slept. He placed Andvari's ring on his hand, then appeared at my bedside with his bloody dagger.

"'Come,' he said, 'I have need of you.'

"Fearfully I did as I was told and dragged the treasure

Next page: Shape-shifting Andvari the Dwarf
transforms into a great pike

out across the Glittering Heath and beyond to a cavern under a mountain deep in the Mirkwood.

"'You make a good porter, my brother. You've earned your life, but little else. If you turn now and run, I will not slay you. Put this gold from your mind, for it shall never be left unguarded.'

"So it was that Fáfnir won the ring and the treasure of the dwarf Andvari with the blood of our father. Over that treasure, he ever after brooded. Hateful lust has poisoned his heart and mind, and all who have come his way by chance or intent he has murdered. For now his outward form has matched his inner evil, and he has become a serpent: a huge dragon, the mightiest of this or any age."

SIGURD AND THE DRAGON

"Slay me this dragon to avenge my father, and win for yourself great glory," commands Regin. "Help me to my share of the weregild, and besides glory you shall have Andvari's ring and the greater part of the treasure, as well."

Sigurd now sees his destiny and takes up Regin's challenge.

For such a mission, the valiant Sigurd desires a weapon to match his strength, and so goes to his mother and claims the shards of his father's sword that had been the gift of Odin. These shards he gives to Regin in his smithy. Regin sets furiously to work, heating them in the hottest fire, re-forging the blade and tempering it in the blood of a bull. The sacred runes above the hilt recover their brightness, the rings engraved on the steel gleam like silver, and as the

Opposite: Sigurd the Dragon-Slayer

smith carries the sword out into the daylight, it seems that flames play along its edge.

Sigurd takes the weapon in his strong hands and swings it fiercely at the smith's anvil. The sword slices clean through the iron and the wooden stock below it, as well. Yet the blade is unnotched by the stroke.

"This truly can be no other but the sword called Gram, the gift of Odin, which my father swore would one day be re-forged and be given to his only son," says Sigurd, smiling.

So armed and mounted on his steed Grani, Sigurd rides on his quest with Regin. They come at last to the fire-scorched and desolate outlands of what was once the Glittering Heath. This place is a wild and blasted heath on the edge of the evil forest of Mirkwood. It is a scorched wasteland where many a hero has been slain by the dragon. Upon this heath is cut a deep path of stone that is the slime-filled track of a dragon road. The road leads to Fáfnir's serpent cavern deep in the Mirkwood. There the dragon made his bed upon the golden treasure that was the ring-hoard of Andvari the Dwarf. Fáfnir left his golden bed only once each day, when he travelled his road to the foul pool on the heath where he drank at dusk.

"Dig a trench in the dragon's path and hide in it," advises Regin. "When he comes over you thrust your sword up into his soft belly. You cannot fail."

While Sigurd is digging, Regin makes off across the heath and hides himself in the Mirkwood. A shadow falls over the pit and Sigurd whirs around. It was the same one-eyed, bearded old man who had given Sigurd his grey horse.

"Small wisdom, short life," murmurs the old man, leaning on his spear. "The dragon's blood will sear your skin. Dig several pits and hide in the one in the left. There you may thrust your blade into the worm's heart, while the boiling, poison blood falls into another pit."

By evening the work is done, and just in time. The stinking dragon comes down to drink, roaring horribly and slavering poison over the ground. Biding his time, Sigurd thrusts Gram's blade into the dragon's breast up to the hilt. The scalding, corrosive blood floods into the ditch, and Fáfnir collapses. His writhing coils shake the earth. His roaring fills the air with flame and venom. His jaws snap at an enemy he cannot reach, as he curses the hero who has slain him and the brother who betrayed him.

When Sigurd emerges from his pit, Regin too comes from his hiding place and feigns both sorrow and joy. Claiming that he wishes to remove any blood guilt from Sigurd for the slaying of Fáfnir, Regin asks Sigurd to cut the dragon's heart from its body and roast it. Regin claims that, by eating the dragon's heart, he alone might be brought to account for its death.

Sigurd does as Regin tells him and builds a fire and spits the heart over the flames. But as the dragon's heart cooks, its juice spits out and scalds the young man's fingers. He puts his fingers in his mouth and, upon tasting the monster's heart-blood, at once finds he can understand the language of the birds in the trees about him.

The birds speak with sorrow, for they know of Regin's treachery. How the smith will gain great wisdom and bravery by eating the dragon's heart, how he then plans to slay Sigurd in his sleep. The birds know that Regin will never share the golden treasure, nor the ring with the brave youth, despite his sworn oath. They know as well that Regin wishes to steal Sigurd's sword and steed.

Hearing this talk among the birds, Sigurd moves swiftly. With his sword, Gram, he strikes the false smith's head from his shoulders. Then, Sigurd eats the dragon's heart himself and sets to work clearing out Fáfnir's lair.

It is a whole day's work, for the cave floor is carpeted with drifts of gold. No three horses could have stood beneath such a load, but Grani carries this with ease. The extra burden of Sigurd, now wearing golden armour, seems to require no effort at all.

So, laden with the Ring of Andvari on his hand, Sigurd the Dragonslayer goes out of that burned wasteland in search of more adventures. He seeks and achieves further honour, for he makes war on all the kings and princes who murdered his father and his kinsmen, and slays them every one.

THE RESCUE OF BRYNHILD

Many other adventures the youth has as well, but then he goes south into the lands of the Franks. Travelling long one night he sees, like a beacon, a great ring of flames on a mountain ridge. The next morning he climbs that ridge called the Hindfell, where he sees a stone tower in the midst of the ring of flames. Sigurd doesn't hesitate. He urges Grani into the ring of fire. Grani does not flinch. His leap is as high as it is long, and though his tail and mane are scorched, he stands quietly once they are through. There is an inner circle next: an overlapping ring of massive war shields, their bases fixed in the mountain rock. Sigurd draws Gram and shears a path through the iron wall of shields. Beyond this is a stone tower, and within it is the body of a warrior on a bier. Or so it seems.

When Sigurd takes the helmet from the warrior's head, he sees that this is a woman and that she is not dead, but sleeping. As he gazes on her, Sigurd sees she is of a warrior's stature and a woman's grace. He also sees a buckthorn protruding from her neck. When Sigurd draws it out, this sleeping beauty sighs and wakes. The shield maiden's steady grey eyes look up at him with love.

This sleeping woman is Brynhild, who was once a Valkyrie, one of Odin's own battle maidens – his beautiful angels of death – who gathered the souls of heroes as they fell in war and carried them to Valhalla. But she once set her will against Odin in the matter of a man's life. For this, Odin pierced her with a sleep-thorn and set her in a tower surrounded by a ring of fire.

Only a hero who did not know fear would be able to pass through the ring of fire. When Brynhild opens her eyes, she knows Sigurd for the hero he is, and Sigurd knows that in the Valkyrie he has his match for courage and his master in wisdom.

When Sigurd becomes the Valkyrie's lover, within the ring of fire, he learns what twenty lifetimes might never teach a mortal man. For in that embrace of love, many things in Sigurd are awakened and he is filled with the wisdom of the gods; while in Brynhild many things are put to sleep, and filled with the unknowing of mortals.

Sigurd, as the lover of the Valkyrie, knows that he must embrace strife and war, which give a warrior immortal fame. Painful as it is, Sigurd knows he must leave Brynhild and go out of the ring of fire into the world of men again, where he might earn glory enough to be worthy of his bride. This Sigurd resolves to do, but as a token of his eternal love and as a promise of his return, he places the Ring of Andvari – that all the world desired – upon Brynhild's hand. While Brynhild sleeps, Sigurd rises at dawn, mounts Grani and passes out of the ring of fire.

When Brynhild wakes, she remembers nothing of Sigurd, or Odin, or any of her past before that day. Upon her hand is a gold ring, though she does not know its reason. All she knows is that she must await the coming of a warrior who knows no fear and can pass through the ring of fire. To this man, and this man alone, she will be sworn in marriage.

IN THE LAND OF THE NIBELUNGS

As for Sigurd, great though his love is for Brynhild, he knows that his fate is that of a warrior. Like his father, he has been chosen by Odin, and in his service Sigurd travels to many lands, and slays no less than five mighty kings in battle. In time, Sigurd comes to the Rhinelands, which are ruled over by the king of the Nibelungs. The Nibelung king welcomes the now famous hero, Sigurd the Dragonslayer, with great warmth and friendship. In time, Sigurd and the king's three sons – Gunnar, Hogni and Guttorm – become the closest of friends and allies in both war and peace. Sigurd and Gunnar swear unbreakable oaths of friendship, and become blood-brothers.

Seeing how Sigurd the Dragonslayer's friendship has so increased the power and wealth of their realm, Gunnar's mother, Grimhild, the queen of the Nibelungs, wishes to keep him within their realm. To this end, she hopes Sigurd might marry her daughter, the beautiful Gudrun. However, although she knows Gudrun loves Sigurd, she also knows Sigurd loves another.

Grimhild's wish is not hopeless. For Grimhild, queen of the Nibelungs though she is, is also secretly a great witch capable of casting spells and making powerful potions. So in the feasting-hall one evening, Grimhild gives to Sigurd an enchanted drink. This potion robs Sigurd of his memory of the Valkyrie whom he swore to love always, and at the same time fills him with desire for the beautiful Gudrun.

Obedient to the spell, Sigurd soon asks for Gudrun's hand and their marriage is blessed by all who live in the Rhinelands. Many seasons pass, the royal couple are happy, and the power and glory of the Nibelungs grows and grows. Yet tales of a strange and beautiful maiden held captive in a ring of fire on a mountain reach the court. These tales mean nothing to Sigurd, but Gunnar wishes to win this maiden and make her his queen. His mother, Grimhild, is wary of this adventure and asks Sigurd to go with his blood-brother. Sigurd does this gladly, but Grimhild also gives to Sigurd a potion. By the potion's power Sigurd may change his appearance to that of Gunnar.

Gunnar and Sigurd ride away and at last come to Hindfell and the mountain with the tower ringed in fire. Gunnar sets his spurs to his horse, but the beast turns away at each attempt, and the flames rear higher and more fiercely at every failure. Even though Sigurd lets him mount Grani, Gunnar gets nowhere.

Gunnar despairs at ever winning his queen, so he begs Sigurd to try in his place. Sigurd uses Grimhild's potion and changes his appearance to that of Gunnar. He then mounts Grani and charges straight into the ring of fire. Sigurd's boots catch fire and Grani's mane and tail are alight. Horse and rider seem to hang in that inferno forever, deafened and blinded by its heat, but finally they pass through the flames.

Next is the barrier of the wall of shields, but as before, Sigurd shears through the iron wall with his sword. Behind this wall in the tower sits the beauty that is Brynhild all in white upon a crested throne, like a proud swan borne up on a foaming wave.

"What man are you?" asks Brynhild of the one standing before her. Memories of her past are gone from her mind, yet something deep within her tells her that something is wrong.

"My name is Gunnar the Nibelung," says the rider, "and I claim you as my queen." Passing through the ring of fire was the price of Brynhild's hand, and she cannot refuse such a hero. Nor is there any reason for her to do so, for the man before her is handsome enough, and – by virtue of his deed – is brave beyond the measure of other mortals.

So Brynhild embraces him and places her gold Ring of Andvari upon his hand to pledge her eternal love. Then within the tower she takes him to bed and lays with him for three nights, although these nights are strange to her. For each night the hero places his long sword on the bed between them. He must do this, he says, for he will not make love to his new queen until they both return to the great halls of the Nibelungs. In this way, the disguised Sigurd conspires, so he might not betray Gunnar and dishonour his bride.

When the marriage of Brynhild and Gunnar takes place in the hall of the Nibelungs, it is the true Gunnar who weds Brynhild and takes her to bed. In the land of the Nibelungs all seems content. But one day while bathing in a stream the two young queens set to quarrelling. Brynhild boasts that Gunnar is a greater man than Sigurd by virtue of his feat of passing through the ring of fire.

Gudrun will have none of this, for Sigurd has foolishly told his wife the true tale of that adventure. So, the young queen cruelly reveals that truth to Brynhild, and, as proof, shows her the gold ring upon her hand. By this Brynhild is crushed, for this was the Ring of Andvari that she thought she had given to Gunnar that day on the mountain, but in fact Sigurd had taken it and given it to his own wife.

BRYNHILD'S REVENGE

Now all the secrets are out, and poison runs in Brynhild's heart when she learns of how she has been deceived. Outraged, she can only think of vengeance. Brynhild turns to Gunnar and his brothers Hogni and Guttorm. She taunts and threatens her husband.

"All the people now laugh and say I have married a coward," mocks Brynhild. "And my disgrace is your disgrace, for they say not only did another man win your wife for you, but also took your place in the wedding bed. And no use is there to deny this, for the Ring of Andvari – which Sigurd gave your sister – is proof that this is so."

"Sigurd shall die, then. Or I shall," swears Gunnar. But he has neither the heart nor the courage to act himself and slay his friend. Instead, he and Hogni inflame the heart of their youngest brother, Guttorm, with promises and Grimhild's potions, to slay Sigurd.

That night Guttorm creeps into the chamber where Sigurd lies sleeping in Gudrun's arms. Young Guttorm thrusts his sword down with such force that it pierces the man and the bedstead too. Waking to death, Sigurd still finds strength enough to snatch up Gram and hurl it after his killer. The terrible sword in flight severs the youth in half as he reaches the door. Guttorm's legs fall forward, but his torso drops back into the room.

When Brynhild hears Gudrun's scream she laughs aloud, but there is no joy in her terrible revenge. For that night, Brynhild takes Sigurd's sword and slays herself. True to her Valkyrie passion, she resolves that, if she cannot be wed to Sigurd in life, she will be wed to him in death. Once again, Sigurd and Brynhild lie side by side – with Odin's bright sword between them – as the fierce flames of their funeral pyre slowly devour them.

GUDRUN AND ATLI

So ends the life of Sigurd the Dragonslayer, but this is not the end of the tale of the Ring of Andvari, nor of the Dwarf's treasure. For the ring remains on Gudrun's hand and the treasure is taken by her brothers Gunnar and Hogni, and hidden by them in a secret cavern beneath the River Rhine.

Gudrun is filled with horror at Sigurd's death at the hands of her brothers, but she does not grieve long before her mother Grimhild comes to comfort her.

Once again, the old witch has prepared a potion, which secretly she gives to Gudrun to make her forget her grief, and the evil her brothers have done. Instead, the potion fills her with love and loyalty to her brothers in all matters. Still, Gunnar and Hogni wish to have Gudrun gone. They also wish to increase the power and glory of the Nibelungs, and believe they might do so by an alliance with the mighty Atli, the King of the Huns. And so, the brothers send Gudrun to Atli. Gudrun likes it not, but obeys and weds the king of the Huns and is his queen.

Now Atli the Hun is a powerful man, but one who is filled with greed. He has heard much of the huge treasure that Sigurd the Dragonslayer once won, and that the Nibelungs have taken this hoard by a foul murder. Each time Gudrun walks before Atli, her gold ring glints and Atli finds that he can think of nothing else but that golden treasure.

THE SLAUGHTER OF THE NIBELUNGS

Time passes and Gudrun gives the Hun king two young sons, but all the while Atli plans an intrigue and finally he acts. King Atli invites Gunnar and Hogni and all the Nibelung nobles to a great feast in his mead hall. But when the Nibelungs come to the feast hall, they soon discover that a huge army of Huns has surrounded them. The great feast hall becomes a slaughterhouse. Although the Nibelungs slay ten for every one they lose, finally they are overwhelmed and all are murdered, save the brothers Gunnar and Hogni. These two are bound with chains and held captive.

The Hun king has Gunnar brought before him in chains and promises to spare his life if he will give up the golden treasure that was taken from Sigurd the Völsung. But Gunnar says that he and Hogni have hidden the treasure in a secret cavern beneath the Rhine, and have sworn blood oaths that neither will reveal it while the other lives. At once, Atli gives an order, and within the hour a soldier returns. In his hand is Hogni's heart, which has been torn from his living breast.

Gunnar greets this loathsome act with cruel laughter. There had been no oath, he explains. Gunnar had been fearful that Hogni might surrender the treasure to save his life. But now that his brother is slain, only Gunnar knows the secret, and he will never surrender it. In rage, Atli has Gunnar bound and cast in a pit where serpents filled with venom finally still that warrior's stubborn heart.

The Hun king's wife, Queen Gudrun, is filled with grief at the death of her brothers and the obliteration of the Nibelungs. Although Andvari's treasure is lost, Andvari's ring still carries the dwarf's curse while it remains on Gudrun's hand. And Gudrun – as the last of the Nibelungs – resolves to have bloody retribution for Atli's treachery.

GUDRUN'S REVENGE

Though the battle with the Nibelungs cost Atli dearly and profited him little, the Hun king calls for a victory feast in his great hall. Secretly, Gudrun makes her preparations. She murders her own two children, Atli's sons. From their skulls, she makes two cups. Their innocent blood she mixes with the wine; and their hearts and entrails she spits and roasts as his meat. All this she serves up to Atli at the feast.

Then, late that night, Gudrun takes a knife and cuts the Hun king's throat while he sleeps. She then creeps away, bars all the doors from without, and sets the Hun king's great hall to the torch. This is the greatest pyre that has ever been seen in the land of the Huns, for all Atli's soldiers and vassals perish in their sleep in that fire.

Before that inferno, Gudrun stands and stares with mounting madness, the flames bringing back many terrible memories. She flees the Hunlands and wanders until she comes to a high cliff overlooking the sea. She looks one more time at the glinting gold Ring of Andvari on her hand, then, with a sigh, she fills her apron with stones and leaps into the sea.

PART

FIVE

ARTHURIAN
LEGENDS

I n *The Lord of the Rings*, Tolkien's heroes Aragorn and
Gandalf are most commonly linked in the popular
imagination with the tales of King Arthur and Merlin
the Magician. This is in part because King Arthur is without
doubt Britain's most famous legendary hero. The stature
of Arthur through many popular retellings has made him
the very embodiment of British virtues and strengths.

English-language readers of *The Lord of the Rings*
frequently register the undeniable connection between
Arthur and Aragorn, and Merlin and Gandalf. However,
what is often not clear to many is that the Arthurian
romances are themselves largely based on earlier Teutonic
myths and legends.

THE ARCHETYPAL HERO

Although the archetypal figures of hero and wizard are clearly
similar in pagan saga, medieval legend and modern fantasy,
the context for all three is very different. The creation of a
medieval King Arthur and a court based roughly on Christian
moral principles naturally resulted in considerable reshaping
of many of the fiercer aspects of the early pagan hero
tradition. The saga hero Sigurd is a wild beast of a warrior,
who clearly would not even get a dinner invitation
to Arthur's courtly Round Table.

Curiously, although Tolkien's world is a pagan,
pre-religious one, his hero requires quite as much reshaping
as Arthur because of his concept of absolute good and evil.
Although Tolkien's Aragorn is a pagan hero, he is often
even more upright and moral than the medieval Christian
King Arthur.

Opposite: Merlin the Magician, King Arthur's mentor,
adviser and chief strategist

The comparison of the three heroes – Arthur, Sigurd and Aragorn – demonstrates the power of archetypes in dictating aspects of character in the heroes of legend and myth. If we look at the lives of each of these three, we see certain life patterns that are identical.

Arthur, Sigurd and Aragorn are all orphaned sons and rightful heirs to kings slain in battle. All are deprived of their inherited kingdoms and are in danger of assassination. All are the last of their dynasty, and their noble lineage will end if they are slain. All are raised secretly in foster homes under the protection of a foreign noble who is a distant relative. Arthur is raised in the castle of Sir Ector; Sigurd in the hall of King Hjalprek; and Aragorn in the house of Master Elrond Half-elven. During their fostering – in childhood and as youths – all three achieve feats of strength and skill that mark them for future greatness.

All three heroes fall in love with beautiful maidens, but all must overcome several seemingly impossible obstacles before they may marry: Arthur to Guinevere, Sigurd to Brynhild, Aragorn to Arwen. Each of these lovers is to some degree a tragic heroine: Guinevere becomes a nun and dies in a convent; Brynhild loses her supernatural Valkyrie power and commits suicide; and Arwen sacrifices her Elven immortality and dies a human death.

FALSE OATHS, FALSE RINGS

In *The Lord of the Rings*, the One Ring is evil; in the *Völsunga Saga*, the Ring of Andvari is cursed. In the Arthurian tradition, the gold ring is good so long as the oath sworn

Opposite: Three Kings: Aragorn, Arthur and Sigurd the Völsung

on it is true. However, whatever the origin of the rings, false oaths sworn on them do not go unpunished.

The Völsung and Nibelung downfalls result directly from Sigurd's unwitting violation of the oath he swore to Brynhild when he gave her the Ring of Andvari as a pledge of eternal love. When Sigurd unknowingly breaks that oath, disaster consumes them all. Similarly, the breaking of the sacred oath sworn on the marriage ring of Arthur and Guinevere – through the queen's adultery with Sir Lancelot – results in the break-up of the Round Table. The iron ring of the knights is broken. Chaos and anarchy are let loose, and the kingdom destroyed. Both traditions read the curse of the ring in the same way: the house built on a lie cannot survive.

The Lord of the Rings follows a similar theme of deceit and false oaths. This is especially the case when Sauron, a master of disguise, goes among the Elven-smiths of Eregion with many false promises about creating rings of virtue and enchantment. So completely does Sauron deceive the Elves that, unknowingly, they help him forge the Rings of Power. Using all the false promises and lies invented by sorcerers since the dawn of time, Sauron forges the One Ring with which he seeks to fetter and enslave the world. When the One Ring is destroyed in the fires of Mount Doom, the illusion of Sauron's power vanishes. Sauron's "house" in the form of the Dark Tower is built on the monstrous lies of the One Ring and cannot survive. The foundations crumble.

THE HERO'S SWORD

Beyond the ring quest motif itself, there are many other points of comparison between the saga, the romance and the

Opposite: Vilya, the "Ring of Air", adorned with a great sapphire-blue stone

fantasy. Tolkien's hero Aragorn in many ways resembles both Arthur and Sigurd, and in some ways, only one or the other.

The heritage of the sword of the warrior king is, naturally enough, critical to all three heroes. Arthur proves his right to the sword in a famous contest: he alone is able to pull the sword from the stone. This is an act that duplicates the contest in the *Völsunga Saga*, when Sigurd's father, Sigmund, can draw the sword Odin has driven into the great oak tree known as the Branstock. However, neither Sigurd nor Aragorn are presented with such contests. They are both given their swords as heirlooms; their problem is that both swords are broken, and neither may use the swords and reclaim their kingdoms until they are re-forged. In Sigurd's case, the sword was broken by the wizard Odin in his father Sigmund's last battle, while Aragorn's sword was broken by his ancestor Elendil in his last battle with the necromancer Sauron.

Like the heirloom swords of Sigurd and Aragorn, Arthur's sword is supposedly unbreakable; but, through special circumstances, all three are broken. Sigmund's and Aragorn's swords break in battles with supernatural opponents, while King Arthur's sword breaks when he makes an unrighteous attack on Sir Pellinore. It seems the Christian king's sword is endowed with a moral conscience. Sir Pellinore is on the point of killing Arthur when Merlin appears and puts Pellinore into a deep swoon. Thus, Arthur's weapon is broken, but he is not slain as Sigmund was when his weapon broke. Arthur is saved by the wizard Merlin; he undergoes a spiritual resurrection. The penitent and reformed Arthur is reborn, as – in a sense – Sigmund is resurrected in his son Sigurd, and Elendil is resurrected in his descendant Aragorn.

Once Sigurd re-forges his sword, Gram, he sets out at once to reclaim his heritage. He does this by avenging his father's death and reclaiming his kingdom by conquest, slaying the dragon Fáfnir and winning the monster's treasure and golden ring. Sigurd then goes on to win his beloved Valkyrie princess Brynhild. To some degree, although the ring quest is different (the aim being destruction rather than winning), Aragorn's life mirrors Sigurd's. Once Aragorn's sword Andúril is re-forged, he sets off to reclaim his heritage. He avenges his father's death, reclaims his kingdom by conquest, and, after the destruction of the One Ring, wins his beloved Elven princess Arwen.

THE HERO'S MENTOR

Perhaps the most telling connection between the three heroes is displayed in the similarity of their mentors: Merlin, Odin and Gandalf. All to some degree fit the archetypal form of the wizard. All are non-human beings gifted with supernatural powers and prophetic skills. All are counsellors of future kings in peace and war, yet have no interest in worldly power themselves. In a sense, they are all vehicles of fate who guide the hero. All are similar in appearance: old yet vital wanderers of great learning with long white beards. They all carry a wizard's staff and wear a broad-brimmed hat and long robes.

In many aspects of his personality, Gandalf is rather more like Merlin than Odin. Odin was, of course, an immortal god who went among the mortals of Midgard as an ancient traveller. Originally, Merlin was in all likelihood an old Celtic god, who similarly visited mortals in this wizard form, although later traditions claimed he was the offspring of a mortal and an elf or demon. Gandalf in origin is a Maia who is chosen as one of five Istari, or Wizards, who come to Middle-earth to live among the mortals.

Next page: Gandalf the Grey topples into the abyss of Moria, only to arise again with greater power as Mithrandir, the White Wizard

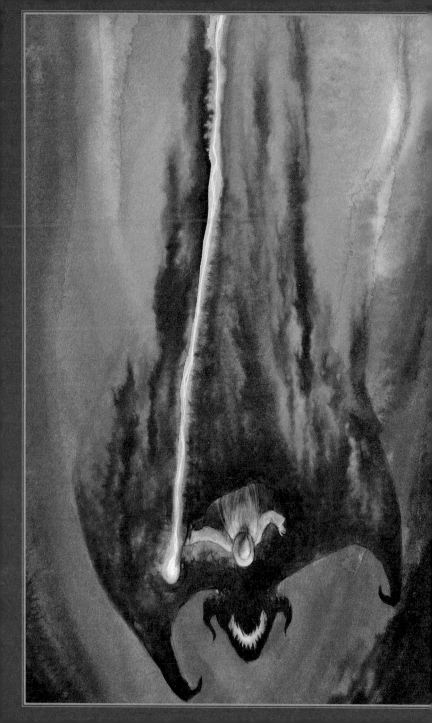

In many of his powers, however, Gandalf is far more like the Nordic Odin than the Celtic Merlin. To begin with, his name comes from the *Prose Edda*, and literally means "sorcerer-elf". In his use of runes, incantations and even his Wizard powers, Gandalf is more comparable to Odin. Even Gandalf's horse comes directly from Norse traditions: Shadowfax means "silver-grey" and closely resembles Grani, "the Grey", the steed of Sigurd. Grani, who understood human speech, was the silver-grey offspring of Odin's supernatural eight-legged horse, Sleipnir. Shadowfax, who also understands the language of Men, is one of the Mearas, a race of horses descended from Nahar, the supernatural horse of the Vala Oromë the Hunter.

Once their work as mentors and advisers to the heroes is done, all three wizards – Odin, Merlin and Gandalf – mysteriously depart. They all pass out of mortal realms rather than die. Odin, after advising his heroes, wanders out of the mortal world, and (after a pilgrimage to Hel) finally ascends the Rainbow Bridge to the immortal kingdom of the gods in Asgard. Merlin wanders away on a solitary pilgrimage, never to return, for he is caught up in an enchantment and lives in a dreaming trance in – according to varying traditions – a tomb, a tree or a tower on an island in the Western Sea.

Tolkien's Gandalf takes elements from both Odin's and Merlin's tales by having a double fate. As Gandalf the Grey, after his battle with the Balrog of Moria, he falls into the bowels of the earth where he remains in a deathlike, yet dreaming, state. When he is resurrected as Gandalf the White, he meets his second end on Middle-earth, when he sails on an Elven ship to the immortal kingdom of the Valar in Aman over the Western Sea.

Opposite: Shadowfax on the Plains of Rohan

THE PASSING OF HEROES

———◆———

The end of Gandalf on Middle-earth with the departure of the Ringbearers in the white Elven ship from the Grey Havens is also the end of Tolkien's epic novel. In looking for Arthurian elements in *The Lord of the Rings*, there can be no doubt that the novel's bittersweet ending is consciously modelled on the tales of Arthur's death. It is an ending that is derived from the Celtic side of Arthurian tradition, rather than its Teutonic one. After his final battle, the mortally wounded Arthur is taken on a mysterious barge by a beautiful faerie queen. The barge carries the wounded king westward across the water to the faerie land of Avalon, where Arthur will be healed and given immortal life.

This end to Arthur's mortal life is very like the end of *The Lord of the Rings*. However, it is important to point out that this is not Aragorn's end. Aragorn remains to die within the mortal world. The supreme reward of this voyage into the land of immortals is reserved for another. The "wounded king" who sails on the Elf queen Galadriel's ship across the Western Sea, past the Elven towers of Avallónë, is not Aragorn. It is Frodo the Hobbit Ring-bearer, who is rightly the real hero of *The Lord of the Rings*.

Curiously, *The Lord of the Rings* and *The Hobbit* move away from the idea of the explicitly mighty and powerful heroes presented in other legends. Although they appear to be a comic foil to the larger heroic personalities of the Men and Elves, nearly all the greatest deeds are achieved, or are caused to be achieved, by the Hobbits. For example, Bilbo's adventures result in the death of Smaug the Dragon and he also finds the One Ring. Samwise mortally wounds the giant

Shelob the Spider, and, most important of all, Frodo (with Gollum) destroys Sauron and the One Ring in Mordor.

March of the Ents on Isengard

PART
·
SIX

CAROLINGIAN LEGENDS

n mainland Europe the historical figure of the Holy Roman Emperor Charlemagne grew into one of the great figures of romance. As with Arthur's knights, Charlemagne's legends included the many tales of his paladins. The adventures of these Christian knights allied to Charlemagne were told in the famous *chansons de geste* ("songs of heroic deeds").

RECREATING AN EMPIRE

Tolkien himself often pointed out how many readers saw the connection between Aragorn and King Arthur, but he found that they usually missed the connection between Aragorn and Charlemagne. Certainly, it seemed to him, Aragorn's great task of forging the Reunited Kingdom of Amor and Gondor from the ruins of the ancient Dúnedain Empire, after more than a millennium of barbarian chaos, was historically parallel to Charlemagne's task of creating the Holy Roman Empire from the ruins of the ancient Roman Empire.

Geographically, as well, Tolkien saw that the extent of the Reunited Kingdom of his epic far more closely paralleled the expanse of Charlemagne's realm. The action of *The Lord of the Rings* takes place in the northwest of Middle-earth, in a region roughly equivalent to the European landmass. Hobbiton and Rivendell, as Tolkien often acknowledged, were roughly intended to be on the latitude of Oxford. By his own estimations, this put Gondor and Minas Tirith some six hundred miles to the south, in a location that might be equivalent to Florence.

Certainly, the scale of Charlemagne's undertaking to create a Holy Roman Empire was more like the challenge that faced Aragorn on Middle-earth than that of King Arthur.

Opposite: Aragorn and Éomer Ride to the Lands of the East

The parallel is fairly obvious. In *The Lord of the Rings*, we learn that the once united Númenórean Kingdom is split into the two weakened and deteriorating realms of the north and south, Amor and Gondor. This is comparable to the historical Roman Empire which was split into two weakened and deteriorating realms of the east and the west, Rome and Byzantium. It is certain that Tolkien himself considered such a parallel, writing that he saw Gondor at the time of the War of the Ring as "a kind of proud, venerable, but increasingly impotent Byzantium".

PARALLEL LIVES

Naturally, there are many other ways in which Aragorn and Charlemagne are comparable. Both carry magical, ancestral swords, both have the power to cure with magical herbs, both have wise old mentors, and both marry elf queens.

Aragorn's sword, Andúril – which was forged by Telchar the Smith – is matched by Charlemagne's sword, Joyeuse – which was said to have been forged by Wayland the Smith. However, it does seem curious that the Christian destroyer of the pagan religions should be armed with a sword that was forged by the same smith who made Gram, the weapon of that supreme warrior of Odin, Sigurd the Dragonslayer.

In *The Lord of the Rings*, Aragorn uses the herb Athelas to cure those who are fatally struck down by the Black Breath of the Nazgûl. In the Carolingian legends, Charlemagne was reputed to have been able to cure those struck down by the plague, or "Black Death", by using the herb called sowthistle. In both cases, these herbs worked their magical cures only if administered by the healing hands of kings – as

Opposite: Andúril

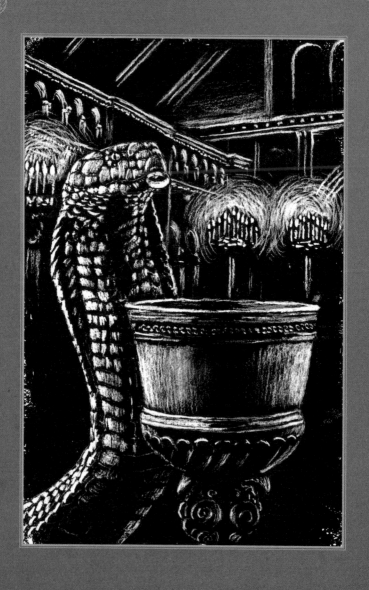

is acknowledged in the folklore of Middle-earth, where the common name for Athelas is kingsfoil.

The key figure of Gandalf the Wizard in *The Lord of the Rings*, as Aragorn's mentor and spiritual guide, cannot properly be transferred into Charlemagne's world. The Church would not allow a wizard as a mentor and spiritual guide to the Holy Roman Emperor. This is especially true as most wizards are to a great extent thinly veiled, earthbound versions of the pagan magician-god Odin/Woden, the Church's greatest enemy.

Consequently, in Charlemagne's Christianized tales, the Gandalf/Merlin/Odin figure is replaced by a wise and elderly churchman. The historical figure of Bishop Turpin supplants the Wizard, and becomes a Christianized version of the same character: the white-bearded, wise old mentor with a bishop's crook instead of a Wizard's staff.

In their choice of queens, Aragorn and Charlemagne are also well matched. Aragorn's betrothal to the Elf princess Arwen is comparable to Charlemagne's engagement, in legend, to the Eastern Elf princess Frastrada.

"THE SERPENT'S RING"

The most compelling of all the Carolingian ring legends is the tale that concerns Charlemagne's marriage to Frastrada. Curiously, this story of Charlemagne and "The Serpent's Ring" is the Carolingian tale that most resembles *The Lord of the Rings* in those elements that relate to the enslaving power of a ring. "The Serpent's Ring" is also the only ring legend that even comes close to Tolkien's moral stance in the rejection of the ring's power. It is also a tale that demonstrates how

Opposite: Enchanted Serpent Ring of Queen Frastrada

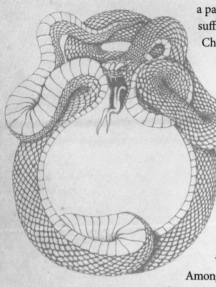

a pagan ring still retained sufficient power in the Christian era to overcome even that most devout hero, the Holy Roman Emperor.

The tale of "The Serpent's Ring" begins on Charlemagne's and Frastrada's royal wedding day. Vassals and peers from all over the world come to the court of Charlemagne with wedding gifts.

Among them is a great serpent with a gold ring in its mouth. The serpent enters the banquet and creeps onto the royal table. There he raises himself up and drops the gold ring from his mouth into a goblet, then turns and slithers out of the banquet hall.

Taking this as a good omen on his wedding day, Charlemagne takes up the ring and places it on the hand of his new queen, Frastrada. However, this serpent ring has a power that Charlemagne has not guessed at, and, once on Frastrada's hand, that power begins to work.

The Serpent's Ring is a ring of enchantment. Charlemagne's love for Frastrada immediately doubles and redoubles. It becomes a compulsive, almost unbearable thing. By its power Charlemagne is irrevocably bound to love and cherish whoever wears the ring. Never can he bear to be parted from the one who has it upon his or her hand.

For a time, all is well, for Frastrada returns Charlemagne's love and the two are happy and the affairs of the kingdom go well. But, after a few years, Frastrada catches a deadly illness, and Charlemagne, even with his healing hands, can do nothing to save her.

Yet when she dies, the spell of the ring does not abate. She is to be buried in a tomb in the cathedral of Mayence, but Charlemagne refuses to be parted from Frastrada and has her laid out in a chamber, where he sits to watch over her body day and night. The power of the ring compels him to see her as beautiful as she was in life. So he remains there day after day, week after week, wasting away and neglecting his empire.

Finally, Bishop Turpin comes to the chamber while Charlemagne lies in a fitful sleep. Like the wise Gandalf who first recognizes the power of the One Ring, it is the old sage Turpin who recognizes the power of the Serpent's Ring. Wishing to release his emperor from the ring's spell, Turpin removes it from the queen's hand and flees from the chamber.

When the emperor awakens, he finds that, although still saddened by Frastrada's death, the savage grief that enslaved him is magically gone. He no longer feels compelled to remain by her side and permits her body to be entombed. However, Charlemagne gradually realizes that he must urgently seek the advice and company of Bishop Turpin. He feels that he had never before realized how important this elderly adviser was to him. It seems to him now that only through his friendship with Bishop Turpin can his life have meaning and purpose.

The emperor immediately rushes to Turpin and declares the bishop the wisest of men and the best of friends. Thereafter, he proclaims, the emperor will never be parted from him, and, in all affairs of state, Turpin's word will hold sway.

Rather daunted by the realization that
the power of the ring can arouse such
love in Charlemagne for a man as well
as for a woman, Turpin nonetheless
takes advantage of its powers so that
he can get Charlemagne to restore his
own health, and then encourages
him to attend to the pressing affairs
of his realm.

This Turpin manages to
achieve, but finally
the bishop
decides he

must reject the power of the ring. Like the Hobbit Frodo in *The Lord of the Rings*, Turpin discovers that the burden of the ring soon becomes too much. However, the old bishop mistrusts its sorcerous power and is fearful lest the ring fall into evil hands. He knows that the emperor will become enslaved and enchanted by anyone who places it on his hand. So, like Frodo, he secretly creeps away into the wilderness and looks for a way of disposing of the ring.

Frodo takes the One Ring to the volcanic fires of Mount Doom in an attempt to neutralize its power. Bishop Turpin finds a remote lake in a forest and throws the ring into its water in his attempt to neutralize its power.

When the bishop returns to Charlemagne the next morning, he finds to his great relief that the emperor's infatuation for him has diminished to the simple comradeship of old. However, that is not an end to the matter. For the Serpent's Ring was not destroyed by being thrown in the lake any more than the One Ring is destroyed when it is lost in the Anduin River. And, as the power of the One Ring called out to Sauron, so the power of the serpent's ring calls out to Charlemagne.

In ways he cannot understand, the ring haunts Charlemagne. His days are restless and his moods will not allow him to concentrate on affairs of state. Full of distraction, he feels compelled to travel and roam distant woodlands. He often calls his huntsmen and wanders the forests of his realm, hoping the chase will dispel his restlessness.

One day Charlemagne enters a particular forest,

Opposite: Tolkien's warlike Southrons of Harad, modelled on Charlemagne's legendary Saracen foes

and feels compelled to go deeper and deeper into its heart, until at last he comes to an open glade, wherein he finds that same lake where Turpin had thrown the ring.

Great joy fills Charlemagne at the sight of the crystal pool. He becomes inexplicably enraptured with the lake in the glade. As he looks on it, his love for this place increases and increases again. He desires nothing so much as to remain in this place all his life.

So it happens that upon this very spot the emperor commands that a great palace and his new court be built. This was how Aix-la-Chapelle (the modern Aachen) became the capital of Charlemagne's realm, for this was where that glade and pool were found, and there the emperor spent most of his days.

It is rather startling to find at the symbolic centre of the realm of the premier Christian monarch a magical pagan ring, jealously guarded by an emperor armed with a magical pagan sword.

This seems a mirror opposite to the original Norse tale of Andvari's Ring, where the greedy dwarf guards a gold ring hidden in a deep pool to keep it from questing heroes. In the Carolingian legend, we have a virtuous emperor guarding a gold ring hidden in a deep pool to keep it from evil pagan powers who come to dethrone him and destroy his empire.

It is also the opposite of the corrupt Gollum in his dark subterranean pool guarding his ring, and of an evil "emperor" like Sauron guarding a gold ring hidden in the Dark Tower to keep it from the good Elvish powers who come to dethrone him and destroy his empire.

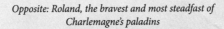

Opposite: Roland, the bravest and most steadfast of Charlemagne's paladins

ROLAND AND OGIER

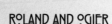

Like King Arthur and his Round Table of knights, Emperor Charlemagne was the focal point of a multitude of *chansons de geste* which concern his loyal paladins. Some aspects of these adventures and their heroes appear to find their way into Tolkien's *The Lord of the Rings*.

One of the most famous of Charlemagne's paladins was the hero Roland. Celebrated in that masterpiece of medieval French literature the *Song of Roland*, this loyal paladin is best known for his famous last stand in the Roncevaux Pass in the Pyrenees against the Saracens. Ambushed and vastly outnumbered, Roland fights valiantly on until his sword breaks. Finally he is overwhelmed by the infidel hordes. As he dies, Roland blows his horn to warn Charlemagne of the attack.

In *The Lord of the Rings*, this event is comparable to the last stand of Boromir, heir to the Ruling Steward of Gondor, in his battle with the Orcs on Amon Hen above the Falls of Rauros. Ambushed by Orcs below the Hill of the Eye, Boromir blows his horn. Though he slaughters a score of Orcs in defence of the Hobbits, he is overwhelmed. His sword is broken and his great horn smashed. Aragorn, like Charlemagne, rushes to the sound of the horn but, like Charlemagne, he reaches his valiant friend too late. Boromir speaks only a few words before he dies.

Another of Charlemagne's great paladins was the hero whom the Danes praise above all other Christian knights. This was Ogier the Dane. The son of King Geoffrey of Denmark, Ogier and his deeds were celebrated in *chansons de geste* and many other legend cycles. In the 19th century, William Morris wrote of Ogier the Dane in his epic poem *The*

Earthly Paradise. As Holger Danske, Ogier is today still the national hero of Denmark.

Ogier the Dane was numbered among the greatest knights of the world. He knew the courts of Charlemagne, of Arthur, of the Langobards, the Huns and Saracens, and embarked on adventures that took him to Jerusalem and Babylon. In his hundredth year, Ogier embarked on one last quest on his return from Jerusalem. He travelled to an isle where a great castle was made of lodestone that tore all iron from ships attempting to sail near its shores. Ogier's ship was wrecked,

Boromir, Faramir and Denethor the Ruling Steward of Gondor

but he made his way to land. The castle was illuminated by a magical light, and Ogier entered it. There he discovered a great serpent in its central court, who guarded a tree in the garden. Ogier drew his sword Courtain and slew the creature. Beneath the tree was the most beautiful woman Ogier had ever seen, and on her hand was a gold ring.

The maid was none other than the immortal Morgan le Fay, the faerie sister of King Arthur. When Morgan placed the golden ring on the old warrior's hand, Ogier's youth was instantly restored. By its power, Ogier was granted eternal youth and immortal life. Young and golden-haired once more, Ogier went with Morgan on a final voyage across the sea to the distant faerie realm of Avalon.

In this Carolingian ring legend, we find many elements comparable to Tolkien's tales. We have a hero on a ring quest who slays a dragon with an ancestral sword. With the ring he wins his elf princess and immortal life as they sail in a faerie ship to a blessed isle of immortals across the sea. Most importantly, however, in Ogier and Morgan, we have the pattern of Aragorn and Arwen: the marriage of the mortal prince and the immortal princess, who make a choice between mortal and immortal worlds. Ogier and Morgan choose the immortal world, while Aragorn and Arwen choose the mortal one.

Opposite: Aragorn and Arwen Meet Among the Birches at Rivendell

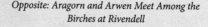

PART
SEVEN

CELTIC
AND SAXON
MYTHS

I n looking for sources for and influences on the imagination
of J. R. R. Tolkien, one must eventually come to the
mythologies of the two great races from whom the British
people are largely descended: the Celts and the Anglo-Saxons.
As a professor of Anglo-Saxon, Tolkien had a great love for
the heroic storytelling traditions of this bold warrior race with
their wonderful epics, chronicles and adventure tales.

BALOR AND THE EVIL EYE

In *The Lord of the Rings* we have Sauron the Evil Eye, the
lord and master of the Orcs, Trolls, Balrogs and most other
monstrous beings. In Celtic myth, we have Balor the Evil Eye,
the king of the monstrous race of deformed giants called the
Formors, who were the chief rivals of the Tuatha Dé Danann
(who are looked at more closely later in this chapter).

The hideous Balor had two eyes: one was normal, but
the other was huge and swollen. He kept the huge eye shut
because it had been filled with such horrific, sorcerous powers
that it virtually incinerated whoever and whatever it looked
upon. In war, Balor took his place in the Formor front line,
facing his enemies while a henchman used a hook to lift his
eyelid and his comrades looked away. In Balor's case, looks
could kill, and any who were within the blaze of his fiery eye
were instantly destroyed.

Many fell to King Balor's Eye until the coming of the
champion of the Tuatha Dé Danann, the golden-haired
warrior Lugh of the Long Arm – Balor's very own grandson.
Seeing the blaze of light just as Balor's eyelid was being lifted
by the hook, the god shot a stone with his rod-sling straight
into the fiery Eye. He hurled the stone with such force that

the Evil Eye was driven right through the back of Balor's skull and into the ranks. There, the blazing Eye incinerated half of Balor's monstrous army and the Formors were driven from the field.

RED BOOKS

When we learn that the most important source of Welsh Celtic lore was preserved in the 14th-century *Red Book of Hergest*, we realize that Tolkien is making a small scholarly joke in naming his "source" of Elf-lore the *Red Book of Westmarch*.

The *Red Book of Hergest* is a manuscript which includes that most important compendium of Welsh legends, *The Mabinogion*. The collection contains many stories of magic rings. The damsel Luned, the Lady of the Fountain, gives a ring of invisibility to the hero Owain. Dame Lyonesse gives her hero, Gareth, a magical ring that will not allow him to be wounded. And Peredur Long Spear goes on a quest for a gold ring, during which he slays the Black Serpent of the Barrows, and wins a stone of invisibility and a gold-making stone.

Tolkien's Elves are largely based on the traditions and conventions of the Celtic myths and legends of Ireland and Wales. However, it is important to understand that, before Tolkien, the "elf" was a vaguely defined concept associated most often with pixies, flower-fairies, gnomes, dwarfs and goblins of a diminutive and inconsequential nature.

TUATHA DÉ DANANN AND SÍDHE

◈

Tolkien's Elves are not a race of pixies. They are a powerful, full-blooded people who closely resemble the pre-human Irish race of immortals called the Tuatha Dé Danann. Like the Tuatha Dé Danann, Tolkien's Elves are taller and stronger than mortals, are incapable of suffering sickness, are possessed of more than human beauty, and are filled with greater wisdom in all things. They possess talismans, jewels and weapons that humans might consider magical. They ride supernatural horses and understand the languages of animals. They love song, poetry and music – all of which they compose and perform perfectly.

The Tuatha Dé Danann gradually withdrew from Ireland as mortal men migrated there from the east. With his ever-present theme of the dwindling of Elvish power on Middle-earth, Tolkien was following the tradition of Celtic myth. The Elves' westward sailings to timeless immortal realms across the sea, while the human race remained behind and usurped a mortal, diminished world trapped in time, recall the diminishing of the Tuatha Dé Danann.

The remnant of this once mighty race was the Aes Sídhe or the Sídhe (pronounced "Shee"). The name means the "people of the hills", for it was believed that these people withdrew from the mortal realm and hid themselves inside the "hollow hills" or within ancient mounds once sacred to them. In Tolkien, as in Celtic legends, we have remnant populations of these immortals in all manner of hiding places: enchanted woods (like Lothlórien), hidden valleys (like Rivendell), in caves (like Menegroth), in river gorges (like Nargothrond) and on distant islands (like Tol Eressëa). Tolkien's Elves, like the Sídhe, seldom intrude on the world

Opposite: The Laiquendi, also known as the Green-elves

of men. They are far more concerned with their own affairs and histories.

Elven time is very different from mortal time: when Tolkien's mortal adventurers pass through an Elven realm they experience a jolt in time, not unlike that of mortals held within their realms by the Sídhe – in extreme cases, sometimes mistaking hours for years, or years for hours. This may be due to the rules of immortality by which both the Elves and the Sídhe are governed.

Both the Elves and the Sídhe are immortal in the same sense that their lifespan is unlimited, but they can be killed. Tolkien follows the Celtic tradition which suggests that immortals cannot survive in a mortal world; that they can remain only at the cost of their powers diminishing. Ultimately, there is a choice between remaining in the mortal world and leaving it forever for another immortal and timeless world beyond the reach of human understanding.

Although Tolkien used elements of Celtic myth in his creation of his Elvish race, his original contribution to these creatures of his imagination is immense and remarkable. Tolkien took the sketchy myths and legends of the Sídhe and the Tuatha Dé Danann and created a vast civilization, history and genealogy for his Elves. He gave them languages and a vast cultural inheritance that was rooted in real history, but flourished in his imagination.

WELSH AND SINDARIN

The degree to which Tolkien's Elves were inspired by Celtic models is most obviously demonstrated by looking at his invented Elvish language, Sindarin. Tolkien himself noted that his invented language and Elvish names of persons and places were "mainly deliberately modelled on those of Welsh (closely similar but not identical)." Structurally and phonetically, there are strong links between the two languages.

A few words are identical: *mal* means "gold" in both the Welsh and Sindar tongues. Others are close: *du* means "black" in Welsh and "shadow" in Sindarin; *calan* means "first day" in Welsh and "daylight" in Sindarin; *ost* means "host" in Welsh and "town" in Sindarin; *sarn* in Welsh means a "stone causeway" and in Sindarin means a "stone" in a ford. There are many others close in spelling and/or meaning: "fortress" is *cacr* in Welsh and *caras* in Sindarin; *drud* in Welsh means "fierce" while *dru* in Sindarin means "wild"; *dagr* in Welsh means "dagger" while *dagor* in Sindarin means "battle". Others are the same words with different meanings: *adan* is "birds" in Welsh and "man" in Sindarin; *nen* is "heaven" in Welsh and "water" in Sindarin; *nar* is "lord" in Welsh and "sun" in Sindarin. Some others are strangely connected: *iar* in Sindarin means "old", while the Welsh *iar* means "hen"; however, the Welsh word *hen* actually means "old". Coincidentally, a few of Tolkien's characters take their names directly from Welsh words: Morwen means "maid", Bard means "poet" and Barahir means "longbeard".

RESTORING ANGLO-SAXON CULTURE

Although the Celts were the older civilization in Britain, it was the Anglo-Saxons who were the dominant race from whom the British inherited most of their language, and consequently most of their culture. Tolkien being a professor of Anglo-Saxon, we can see how his expertise in this area

Wose

Púkel Man

Wudu-wása
(Middle English:
wodwos)

púcel
(Early Modern English:
puckle)

satyr/faun
(wild man
of the woods)

goblin/demon

IN TOLKIEN'S WORK

OLD ENGLISH

ENGLISH

Hobbit

bytla

builder

hol

hole

warhorse

eoh

Éowyn

Meara

méarh

horse

wyn

delight

chief of a nation

Þéoden

demon

orc

giant

þéoden

Théoden

Orc

orc

ent

Ent

ent

ent

influenced his imagination in relation to aspects of his human cultures, as much as that of the Celts influenced his Elves.

It must also be remembered that Tolkien frequently expressed his desire to restore the mythology and literature of early England to the English. By this, he meant the lost mythology and literature of Anglo-Saxon Britain between the time of the Roman retreat in 419 CE and the Norman Conquest in 1066. With the notable exception of *Beowulf* and a handful of poem fragments, the ruthless obliteration of Anglo-Saxon culture by the Norman conquerors was nearly absolute.

In his imaginative writing, Tolkien wished to retrieve something of the atmosphere of that lost age of heroes and dragons. Consequently, we see Anglo-Saxon elements playing a critical part in his writing. His mortals predominantly speak Westron, or the Common Speech of Men, which is "translated" as modern English; however, many of the names and places relating to Men are "translated" as Anglo-Saxon, or Old English. Hundreds of Old English words are employed. Indeed, we find all the Northmen and Rohirrim names (e.g., Éowyn – "horsewoman" – and Théoden – "chief of a nation") are in Old English as the names of the Dwarves are Icelandic, and those of the Elves are rooted in Welsh.

Also, the names Men give to other races are often rooted in Old English. Ent is derived from the Old English for giant, Orc from demon or goblin, Meara from horse, and Hobbit is from invented Old English *Holbytla*, or "hole builder". Wose is derived from *wodwos*, a sylvan goblin. Pukel Men is from *puckle*, meaning goblin or demon, a word which survives in the English folklore figure of Puck, immortalized by Shakespeare.

Opposite: Tolkien's Mannish languages are rooted in Anglo-Saxon (Old English)
Previous Pages: Tolkien's Elvish Sindarin language is modelled on Welsh

BEOWULF AND THE HOBBIT

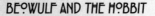

In the Teutonic hero cycles popular among the Anglo-Saxons we can see some elements that undoubtedly influenced Tolkien's writing. This was particularly true in ring-related tales.

The importance of the Völsung ring legend in establishing royal lineage and historic stature can be easily recognized in history and literature throughout Northern Europe. Even in the oldest surviving Teutonic epic, that 8th-century masterpiece of Anglo-Saxon literature, *Beowulf*, the ring legend and its hero Sigurd are discernible.

There is no doubt that the tale of Beowulf was an Anglo-Saxon attempt to rival the greatness of the Völsung hero. Before the scald sings his tribute to Beowulf, he begins by singing first of Sigurd, or Siegmund, as he was known to the Anglo-Saxons. Siegmund is said to be the most famous of all heroes whose greatest deed was the slaying of a dragon and the winning of a ring-hoard.

The scald gives such an abbreviated version of the legend that it is obvious that this was a tale with which everyone listening was expected to be familiar. Furthermore, it is used to foreshadow Beowulf's dragon battle which will win him comparable fame among his own folk.

When Beowulf slays the monster Grendel, he is rewarded with gold finger rings, arm rings and neck rings by King Hrothgar, "Lord of the Ring-Danes". Decades later, Beowulf rules as the Lord of the Ring-Danes in Hrothgar's place, and his last heroic deed is to do battle with a terrible flying fire-breathing dragon that is guardian of a huge ring-hoard of an ancient vanished race.

Tolkien, as a professor of Anglo-Saxon, was an authority on *Beowulf*. The two tales are not very obviously similar; however, there are strong parallels in the plot structure of the dragon episode of *Beowulf* and that of the slaying of Smaug in *The Hobbit*. Beowulf's dragon is awakened by a thief who finds his way into the dragon's cavern and steals a jewelled cup from the treasure hoard. This is duplicated by Bilbo Baggins's burglary in Smaug the Dragon's cavern, when the Hobbit also steals a jewelled cup from the treasure hoard. Both thieves escape detection and the anger of the dragons themselves; however, the nearby human settlements in both tales suffer terribly from the dragon's wrath.

It is up to their respective champions, Beowulf and Bard the Bowman, to slay the beast. This they both do, although Bard survives to become King of Dale, while Beowulf does not. Following the pattern of Siegmund in his last battle, Beowulf's sword, Nailing, breaks, and, although he is victorious, he dies of his wounds. Beowulf's death is mirrored in *The Hobbit* by the other warrior-king of the tale, the Dwarf Thorin Oakenshield, who lives long enough to know that he has been victorious, but dies of his wounds on the battlefield.

ANGLO-SAXON ELEMENTS IN THE LORD OF THE RINGS

Other Anglo-Saxon tales also made major contributions to Tolkien's writings. One certainly was the ring legend of the Saxon hero Wayland the Smith. Wayland's tales were extremely popular during the Middle Ages. He was a Saxon Daedalus and the greatest craftsman of his race. Again, it was a legend with which Tolkien was familiar.

In the Middle Ages, it became traditional for the swords

of great heroes to come from the forge of Wayland the Smith. In the *Nibelungenlied*, Siegfried's sword Balmung was of Wayland's making, as was Charlemagne's blade, Joyeuse. In the *Wilkina Saga*, Wayland forges the sword Mimung or Mimming for his heroic son Witig, but the blade also makes its way to the hero Dietrich von Berne. Wayland is also the sword-maker in the *Waltharius*, for the Saxon hero Walter of Aquitaine.

Most remarkable of all, one Wayland tale claims that after fleeing to the realm of the Elf-smiths of Alfheim, the hero-smith gave his own sword to Odin the Allfather. This was the same sword that Odin takes to Midgard and drives into the tree Branstock: Gram, the fiery sword of the *Völsunga Saga*.

VÖLUNDR: THE CURSED SMITH

In Wayland the Smith we have the figure of the gifted but cursed smith who in Tolkien is manifest in the Noldorin Elf Fëanor, who makes the Silmarils that are later stolen by Morgoth. He is also comparable to Telchar the Smith, the supreme Dwarf-smith who forged the Dúnedain sword inherited by Aragorn, with which Elendil cuts the One Ring from Sauron's hand. Telchar also forged the dagger Angrist, which Beren used in the Quest of the Silmaril to cut the jewel from Morgoth's iron crown. More particularly, however, we can see in the tale of Wayland's ring something of the figure of Celebrimbor, Lord of the Elvensmiths of Eregion, who forged the Rings of Power.

The tale of the ring of Wayland the Smith – known as Wieland to the Germans – comes to us largely through a later Norse version, in which the Saxon hero is called Völundr. This

was written down in the long Icelandic narrative poem, the
Völundarkvitha.

The tale of Völundr begins with his winning of a Valkyrie
wife, who had descended to earth in the guise of a swan
maiden. Völundr captures the plumage of this swan maid,
thus preventing her escape, and in her form as a mortal
woman he takes her as a wife. After nine years the Valkyrie
discovers the hiding place of her plumage and flees the mortal
world. However, as a token of her continued love for him, she
leaves Völundr a magical ring of the purest gold.

The Haunted Barrow-downs of Eriador

By the powers of this ring, Völundr's already formidable skills increase beyond that of all men. Weapons and armour blessed with fantastic powers, and jewels of exquisite beauty and intricacy, come forth from Völundr's forge. Most valued of Völundr's creations are his swords, the best of all being his own sword which always has fire playing around its razor edge. It is a blade that can never be blunted or broken, and any who hold it cannot be defeated in battle.

Völundr's ring is also a source of almost infinite wealth. Placing his ring upon his forge, Völundr pounds out with his hammer seven hundred gold rings of equal weight from its shape. So great is Völundr's wealth that Nidud, the king of Sweden, sends his soldiers to capture the smith and seize his treasures and his magical ring.

The evil king then makes a slave of Völundr. He has the smith crippled by hamstringing him, then exiled to a rocky isle, where he is forced to build a fortress labyrinth that serves as his own prison. Here Völundr is ordered to make jewels, ornaments and weapons for his master's amusement.

After many years, Völundr manages by trickery to avenge himself on Nidud by slaying the king's sons, violating his daughter and regaining his sword and his ring. Völundr then uses his skills to forge a pair of huge wings, much like those of the Valkyrie swan maiden who was once his wife.

With these wings, he flies out of his island prison and far beyond Midgard and the realm of mortal men. He flies to that place called Alfheim, the land of the Elfs, where live the finest smiths in creation. So great is Völundr's skill that the Elf-smiths welcome him as a peer. With the Elfs of Alfheim and the power of the ring, Völundr conceives and fashions many a miraculous work for gods and heroes, greater than any he made in the world of men.

Opposite: Frodo Baggins and the Barrow-wight

VÖLUNDR'S RING AND THE BARROW-WIGHTS

In some lost versions of the legends, Völundr's ring appears to have been stolen in Alfheim by the Dwarf Andvari and taken back into Midgard. There it becomes Andvarinaut, the self-same ring of the *Völsunga Saga*. However, in the surviving versions of the Völundr tale, his ring has another destiny. It does not remain in Alfheim but is stolen by a daring mortal pirate called Sote the Outlaw. After taking the ring, he becomes obsessed with it. Fearful that someone will steal it from him, he flees to Bretland and has himself buried alive in a hollow barrow grave.

In this great mound, with drawn sword and dagger, he wanders the passages, never sleeping, awaiting any who might attempt to take the fabulous ring. Sote the Outlaw becomes a haunted, blasted spirit. Possessed and cursed by the power of the ring, Sote becomes an immortal ring-wraith, one of the living dead that men called barrow-wights, who haunt the graves of men.

Völundr's ring is the object of the quest of hero Thorsten. When Thorsten comes at last to Bretland, he enters the hollow hill that is the barrow grave where Sote the Outlaw hides. The wailing screams of a tortured fiend, the cries of a living man, and the sound of steel striking stone and bone are heard, and the flickering of sorcerous flames can be seen within. Finally Thorsten emerges from the dark passage, pale and bloody as a ghost himself, but in his left hand is the glinting gold of Völundr's ring.

The latter part of the tale of Völundr's ring is certainly a major source for Tolkien for his Hobbits' near-fatal encounter with the barrow-wights of the Barrow-downs. Of course, the difference is that although the barrow-wights had their own

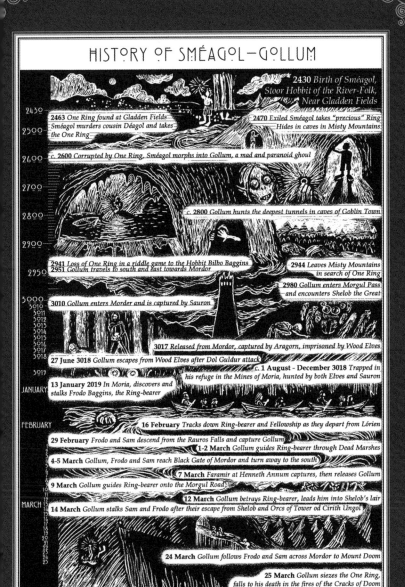

HISTORY OF SMÉAGOL—GOLLUM

2430 *Birth of Sméagol, Stoor Hobbit of the River-Folk, Near Gladden Fields*

2463 *One Ring found at Gladden Fields Sméagol murders cousin Déagol and takes the One Ring*

2470 *Exiled Sméagol takes "precious" Ring Hides in caves in Misty Mountains*

c. **2600** *Corrupted by One Ring, Sméagol morphs into Gollum, a mad and paranoid ghoul*

c. **2800** *Gollum hunts the deepest tunnels in caves of Goblin Town*

2941 *Loss of One Ring in a riddle game to the Hobbit Bilbo Baggins*
2951 *Gollum travels to south and east towards Mordor*

2944 *Leaves Misty Mountains in search of One Ring*

2980 *Gollum enters Morgul Pass and encounters Shelob the Great*

3010 *Gollum enters Morder and is captured by Sauron*

3017 *Released from Mordor, captured by Aragorn, imprisoned by Wood Elves*

27 June 3018 *Gollum escapes from Wood Elves after Dol Guldur attack*

c. **1 August - December 3018** *Trapped in his refuge in the Mines of Moria, hunted by both Elves and Sauron*

13 January 2019 *In Moria, discovers and stalks Frodo Baggins, the Ring-bearer*

16 February *Tracks down Ring-bearer and Fellowship as they depart from Lórien*

29 February *Frodo and Sam descend from the Rauros Falls and capture Gollum*
1-2 March *Gollum guides Ring-bearer through Dead Marshes*

4-5 March *Gollum, Frodo and Sam reach Black Gate of Mordor and turn away to the south*

7 March *Faramir at Henneth Annun captures, then releases Gollum*

9 March *Gollum guides Ring-bearer onto the Morgul Road*

12 March *Gollum betrays Ring-bearer, leads him into Shelob's lair*

14 March *Gollum stalks Sam and Frodo after their escape from Shelob and Orcs of Tower od Cirith Ungol*

24 March *Gollum follows Frodo and Sam across Mordor to Mount Doom*

25 March *Gollum siezes the One Ring, falls to his death in the fires of the Cracks of Doom*

treasures, it was Frodo who possessed the One Ring. Also in Tolkien's tale, it is that odd creation Tom Bombadil who bursts into the barrow grave to scatter the barrow-wights and save the Ring-bearer and his companions.

However, with the introduction of the barrow-wight spirit – in the figure of Sote the Outlaw – we see the concept of a ring that gives mortals immortality and fiendish powers but which also enslaves them and destroys their human souls. Perhaps in Sote the Outlaw there is something of the Witch-king and the Ringwraiths of *The Lord of the Rings* – mortal men who become immortal, blasted spirits through the Rings of Power.

In Sote's paranoid, ghoulish behaviour after he steals the ring, we may also perceive something of the character of Sméagol/Gollum. For after Gollum murders his cousin and steals the One Ring, like Sote he becomes obsessed with this "precious" ring, and, in a kind of miserly madness, he also buries himself alive. In the foul tunnels of an abandoned Orc hold beneath the hills, Gollum hides (like Sote) and murders any who dare to come near, for fear that they might steal his precious ring.

Opposite: Sméagol/Gollum in his deep cavern and
dank pool beneath Goblin Town

PART
EIGHT

GERMAN ROMANCE

The medieval German legend that most resembles the imaginative sweep and dramatic impact of *The Lord of the Rings* is the tale of the hero Dietrich von Berne and Virginal, the Ice Queen of Jeraspunt. There are aspects of this tale that are suggestive of the major themes and characters in both *The Lord of the Rings* and *The Silmarillion*.

Of all the heroes of medieval German romance, Dietrich von Berne is certainly the greatest. This mighty Ostrogoth hero who was also called Dietrich of Verona was, like Arthur and Charlemagne, a central figure around which a large number of hero's stories were told. Also like Charlemagne, Dietrich was based on a real historical figure: in this case, Theodoric the Goth, who eventually became the Roman emperor Theodoric the Great (454–526 CE).

From Tolkien's letters, we know that he was fascinated with the Goths. He felt that surviving fragments of Gothic text combined with reading of Latin historical documents gave him exciting insights into an authentic ancient German culture. And although he was more interested in the historical Theodoric the Goth, he was obviously imaginatively provoked by the adventures of the romantic Dietrich von Berne.

DIETRICH AND THE ICE QUEEN

The tale of Dietrich and the Ice Queen begins with the hero entering the realm of a race of mountain giants ruled over by Orkis the cannibal giant, and his evil son, the wizard Janibas. Dietrich learns that the giants are making war on the highest mountain kingdom of the ice faeries in the snow-peaked Alps. This was the domain of the magical snow maidens who were ruled

Opposite: Morgoth, the Dark Enemy

by Virginal, the Ice Queen, from her glittering ice castle of Jeraspunt, on the highest peak in the Alps. Dietrich carries out a long campaign of war on the mountain giants, slaying one after the other and taking mountain castle after mountain castle. In one titanic battle, he meets and kills the terrible giant Orkis himself.

However, when Dietrich arrives within sight of Jeraspunt, he finds the way barred by the son of the giant king – a foe more formidable than Orkis himself. For the wizard Janibas has laid siege to the shining castle with an awesome army of giants, evil men and monsters. To his foes, Janibas appears as a phantom black rider who commands tempests and is backed by demons and hellhounds. But the wizard's most terrifying power is his ability to command those who were slain in battle to rise up from the dead and fight again. Beyond his ambition to seize the realm of the Ice Queen and her castle, Janibas's main driving desire is to enhance his sorcerer's powers by taking possession of the magical jewel in the crown of the Ice Queen. For by the powers of this jewel she can command the elements of the lands of ice and snow, and by it she rules the mountains.

Dietrich can see the siege army lying like a black sea around the many-towered ice castle. It is obvious that, however well defended, the castle must eventually fall to the never-dwindling numbers of the sorcerer's army. Despite what would seem an impossible task, Dietrich is spurred to a battle frenzy by the sight of the beautiful Ice Queen on the battlements of the tallest tower. Her radiance matches even that of the star-like jewel dancing in her crown with icy light.

In his valiant attempt to raise the siege, Dietrich slaughters all before him, but this proves futile as the dead simply rise up to fight again. Dietrich then decides on another strategy. Seeing that Janibas commands his forces by means of a sorcerer's iron tablet held aloft, Dietrich pursues the black horseman himself. Striking Janibas down from his phantom steed, Dietrich lifts his sword and smashes the iron tablet. As the tablet breaks, the glaciers of the mountains split and shatter, thundering down in massive avalanches that bury the whole evil host of giants and phantoms and undead forever.

Undead battalions of Janibas the Necromancer

Dietrich triumphantly makes his way to the castle as the gates are flung open to greet him. He is welcomed by the incomparable Ice Queen herself, surrounded by her dazzling court of snow maidens, all aglow with fairy light and the glitter of diamond veils. Here in the ice castle of Jeraspunt, in the realm of the ice faeries, Dietrich and the Ice Queen are wed.

In the legend of the Ice Queen, Janibas the necromancer, as the black horseman, is very like a combination of Sauron the Necromancer and his chief lieutenant, the Witch-king, Lord of the Ringwraiths. The One Ring is replaced by an iron tablet, but the climax of the tale reads very like Sauron's ultimate battle at the Black Gate at the end of *The Lord of the Rings*. The result of the destruction of the iron tablet on Janibas's evil legions is identical to the destruction of the One Ring on those of Sauron.

Janibas's father, Orkis, the king of the mountain giants, is very like Sauron's ancient master, Morgoth the Dark Enemy, who rules the evil mountain realm of Angband in *The Silmarillion*. It is interesting to note that the cause of Morgoth's war with the Elves is the star-like Silmaril jewels that Morgoth wears in his Iron Crown. The cause of Orkis's war with the faeries is the star-like jewel that the Ice Queen wears in her crown.

Although the Ice Queen is comparable to the Elf queen Galadriel in her enchanted forest realm of Lothlórien, or even the Elf princess Arwen in Imladris in *The Lord of the Rings*, the siege of the faerie ice castle of Jeraspunt in the middle of the Alps is more like the many-towered Elven city of Gondolin in the middle of the Encircling Mountains in *The Silmarillion*.

THE LANGOBARD AND AMELUNG CYCLES

Although in the tale of Dietrich and the Ice Queen aspects of the ring are taken on by the iron tablet and the star-like jewel, there are many legends of German romance where the ring is overtly the key element. This is certainly true of the Langobard and the Amelung hero cycles.

The fierce Langobards were one of the many powerful Germanic tribes who invaded the eastern European borderlands of the Roman Empire. These warrior people later swept into northern Italy, where they were known as the Lombards, and gave their name to the region called Lombardy in the present day. Described by Latin historians as the supreme horsemen of the Germanic peoples, the Langobards were Tolkien's models for the Rohirrim.

Elven citadel of Gondolin hidden within the Encircling Mountains

Historical accounts of the Langobard cavalry in battle closely resemble the dramatic "Charge of the Rohirrim" in *The Lord of the Rings*.

The hero of the Langobard cycle is Ortnit, who is given a gold ring by his mother that gives him the strength of 12 men. This ring allows him to subdue an innocent-looking, unarmed child blessed with huge physical strength, who has slain scores of knights. Once Ortnit makes this rather embarrassing conquest, it is revealed to him that the child is actually none other than the powerful dwarf king Alberich (the German name for Andvari). He acknowledges that he is the same dwarf of legend and is now more than five hundred years old. Furthermore, the dwarf king reveals that the ring on Ortnit's hand once belonged to him, but he gave it to Ortnit's mother as a token of love, for in truth Alberich is Ortnit's true father.

The dwarf king now joyfully gives his son armour and a sword. The sword, called Rosen, and the armour were both forged by Alberich and tempered in dragon's blood. The sword is unbreakable, and the armour is impenetrable. He also tells him that the ring will not only increase his strength, but can also be used to heal the sick and wounded, and can be used magically to summon Alberich himself. With the sword, the armour and the ring, Ortnit wins fame and riches and becomes king of Lombardy. In the end, however, Ortnit meets his end when two dragons crush him to death. His sword and armour remain in their cavern, but his ring is retained by Alberich, until the coming of a hero who might be a worthy heir to Ortnit.

Dwarf Armour

The heir to the ring emerged in the Amelung hero cycle. The Amelungs were a German tribe who rose to prominence when their warrior king Anzius was crowned emperor of the Eastern Empire in Constantinople. The greatest hero of the Amelung cycle is Wolfdietrich, who is the rightful heir to the emperor. However, abandoned in childhood by his brothers, he is raised by wolves. After many adventures, Wolfdietrich comes to Lombardy, where he is challenged by the dwarf Alberich. Winning a test of strength with Alberich, he is awarded Ortnit's ring and goes on to fight the two dragons of Lombardy. Taking the sword Rosen from Ortnit's dead hand within the cave, Wolfdietrich slays the dragons. The victorious Wolfdietrich is married to Ortnit's widow and becomes king of Lombardy. Armed with the ring, sword and armour, Wolfdietrich raises an army, marches on Constantinople and lays claim to his birthright. He is crowned Emperor of the Eastern Empire, but his destiny is not yet fulfilled. He returns to Lombardy with an even greater army, then marches south to Rome, where he is crowned emperor of the West as well. Once again, the master of the ring reunites an ancient broken empire.

ALBERICH THE DWARF

In the many German hero cycles, the most persistent character in the ring quest tradition is the guardian of the ring and the treasure. This is the dwarf known as Andvari in Norse tales and Alberich in German legends. Although capable of being tamed, he is usually a sinister figure; however, in later romances his appearance and powers often change. He sometimes lends help to other heroes under alternative names: Alferich, Laurin and Elbeghast. Increasingly, this character supplies all the supernatural elements in German romance: dwarf, wizard, elf, smith, guardian and god. By the late 16th century he is entirely transformed, appearing in Shakespeare's *A Midsummer Night's Dream* as Oberon, king of the faeries, whose main business seems to be the orchestration of love affairs. Quite a remarkable evolution from a rather nasty Norse dwarf.

In Tolkien, the Dwarves are often hoarders and guardians of various treasures. However, an equivalent figure to the dwarf Andvari/Alberich in *The Lord of the Rings* is manifest in the strange character of Sméagol/Gollum, the former Hobbit turned into a tormented ghoul by the curse of the One Ring. He is not far off becoming a Ringwraith enslaved by the power of the One Ring, but manages in some perverse Hobbitish way to remain his own creature.

In medieval German romance, the same dwarf of the Langobard cycle of Ortnit and the Amelung cycle of Wolfdietrich reappears in the hero cycles of the Goths. Inevitably, their hero Dietrich von Berne encounters Alberich. Legend dictates that Dietrich von Berne was the great-grandson of the Amelung hero, Wolfdietrich. Dietrich goes into battle with the dwarf king Alberich, who – in this particular manifestation – rules a subterranean kingdom in the Tyrolean mountains. After various intrigues and battles, Dietrich overthrows the dwarf and wins his magical golden ring, a girdle of strength, a cape of invisibility, a vast golden treasure and the sword Nagelring.

Dietrich's exploits as the premier German hero are as extensive as Arthur's and Charlemagne's. His adventures cross over many other ring quest cycles in many rather unexpected ways. Inevitably, the peripatetic Dietrich makes an appearance

in the German people's greatest medieval epic, the
Nibelungenlied. As a liegeman to the Hun Emperor
Etzel, he is reluctantly drawn into the Nibelung
tragedy. He becomes the *deus ex machina* of the epic
tale, and is forced into a position where he must
destroy the last vestige of the Nibelung dynasty.

PART

NINE

THE
NIBELUNGENLIED

No investigation of the theme of the ring quest would be complete without reference to the *Nibelungenlied*. As with the *Völsunga Saga*, the story of this epic will be told in full without interjection or immediate comparison with Tolkien's *The Lord of the Rings*.

The *Nibelungenlied* is the tale of the rivalry of two queens. One is the gentle Queen Kriemhild who, with three brothers, rules the Burgundian kingdom of the Rhine. The other is the warrior-queen Brunhild who alone rules in far Iceland.

RHINELANDS AND NIBELUNGENLAND

Queen Kriemhild's sleep is broken by a prophetic dream. In the dream a falcon is upon Kriemhild's jewelled wrist. This falcon is without equal; it is the most cherished of all things that Kriemhild calls her own. Yet, without warning, two eagles strike the bird in flight. Before Kriemhild's eyes, the eagles tear her falcon to pieces and glut themselves on its flesh.

Young Kriemhild goes to her mother who is a woman wise in the reading of dreams, but the woman can give her child no comfort. The falcon is a prince whom Kriemhild will love and marry, while the eagles are two murderers who would destroy that prince. And so, because of this dream, Kriemhild swears she will wed no man. Though many chivalrous knights desire her and sing her praises, she will wed no one. Nor are there any who might force her to wed, for her will is protected by her three brothers, the powerful kings of the Rhinelands: Gunther, Gernot and Giselher.

Yet fate will not allow Kriemhild to keep her vow. North of the kingdom of the Rhinelands are the Netherlands and the great city of Xanten. There lives the hero Siegfried, the son of King Siegmund and Queen Sieglind. This is the mighty warrior who gained fame by travelling far to the north into the land of the Nibelungs, the richest kingdom in the world. There Siegfried slays the twelve guardian giants of Nibelungenland and takes from their armoury that ancient sword called Balmung, and with it defeats seven hundred men of Nibelungenland. At last he fights the two mighty kings of the Nibelungs themselves and, in the din of combat, slays them both.

Yet the great treasure of the Nibelungs has one last guardian, more subtle and dangerous than all the rest. This is the ancient dwarf Alberich, who not only possesses huge strength but also wears the Tarnkappe, the Cloak of Invisibility. So Siegfried fights an invisible foe, but finally locks the dwarf in his grip, overthrows him, and wins from him both the magic cloak and the Nibelung treasure. So vast was the Nibelung treasure that it would take one hundred baggage wagons to carry away the precious stones alone; though these were but a scattering over the mounds of red-gold that were heaped on the floors of the secret cavern where it was kept.

By force of arms, Siegfried becomes master of the Nibelung treasure and Lord of Nibelungenland. And though Siegfried returns to Xanten to rule the Netherlands, he is acknowledged as the King of Nibelungenland as well. However, this is not the end of Siegfried's deeds, for besides countless combats against other men, this hero also slays a dragon. Further, by this deed Siegfried wins not just fame but invincibility. For after slaying the monster, he bathes in the dragon's blood, and his skin grows tough as horn so that no weapon can pierce him.

When Siegfried rides south in search of adventure, he comes to the land of the Burgundians, and there the three kings of the Rhinelands greet him with honour. For the best part of a year Siegfried remains in the Rhinelands in the great city of Worms and with King Gunther swears an oath of friendship. Still, there is another reason for Siegfried's journey. He has heard of the beauty of Kriemhild, and hopes he might win her as his queen.

Siegfried has reasoned well, for from her tower Kriemhild has often watched the hero in pageant and combat. By the sight of him alone, she is filled at once with love, and her resolve not to give her heart to any man is soon discarded.

THE WOOING OF BRUNHILD

Now Gunther reveals that he is as enamoured by that other beautiful maiden-queen who rules in Iceland as Siegfried is of the fair Kriemhild. The only problem is that Queen Brunhild is no ordinary woman. She is a warrior-queen blessed with supernatural strength, and she swears that she will wed no man unless he can defeat her in three feats of strength.

So the bargain is struck. King Gunther will grant Queen Kriemhild's hand to Siegfried, if Siegfried helps Gunther win the beautiful Queen Brunhild. Siegfried and Gunther set sail for far Iceland.

The travellers are graciously received by the queen upon a throne all wreathed in silk and gold. She is as beautiful as all the tales have claimed. On her hand she wears an ancient red-gold ring, and about her waist is a girdle adorned with precious gems: a splendid orphrey of fine silk braid from Nineveh.

Gunther's heart goes out to Brunhild at once, but it is to Siegfried that Brunhild speaks first. For the queen assumes that Siegfried is the most noble of her visitors, and that it is he who has come as suitor. Here is the first of Siegfried's deceptions. To Brunhild, Siegfried falsely claims that he is a vassal to King Gunther, who is the greatest and strongest of heroes, and it is Gunther who comes to compete for her hand. With some reluctance the queen accepts Gunther's challenge and agrees to the contest.

Queen Brunhild stands alone in the vast arena, surrounded by an iron ring of seven hundred men-at-arms who will judge the contest. The warrior-queen dresses herself in steel armour adorned with gold and gems. It takes four strong men to lift the queen's bright shield, and three men to carry her spear: both of these she takes and wields like childish toys. Then into that arena marches her suitor and challenger, King Gunther of the Rhine. However, though he appears to stand alone against the warrior-queen, this is not so. The wily Siegfried has covered himself in Tarnkappe, his magic cloak, which not only makes him invisible, but has a second power, that of increasing the strength of its wearer twelvefold.

Brunhild is amazed when Gunther does not fall. Instead, Gunther appears to lift up her spear and, turning the blunt end to the fore – so as not to slay the maid – throws the weapon with such force as to drive her to the ground. But here Brunhild is deceived by appearance, for it was the invisible hand of Siegfried which hurled the spear.

Then come the next two tests: the casting of a great stone and the long leap. The stone is so heavy it takes 12 men to carry it into the arena. Without hesitation, Queen

Brunhild lifts the stone and throws it the length of those 12 men laid end to end; then she makes a mighty leap that overshoots the distance of the stone.

In silent reply, Gunther goes to the stone and appears to lift it effortlessly, but once again it is the invisible Siegfried who does the deed and hurls the stone far beyond Brunhild's mark. Then, lifting Gunther by his waist, Siegfried leaps, carrying Gunther with him through the air, landing far beyond their stone-cast.

THE NEWLYWEDS AT WORMS

So, by the strength and cunning of Siegfried, Gunther has won a bride, and to the Kingdom of the Rhine comes the proud Queen Brunhild. In Gunther's court at Worms there is much celebration and joy. There are to be two royal marriages: Gunther to Brunhild and Siegfried to Kriemhild.

Wedding guests are given gifts of bracelets, lockets and rings, while an iron ring of armed knights solemnly stands about the betrothed couples as they swear their holy vows. Joyfully, Gunther and Siegfried march out of the chapel with their brides. As night comes, they retire to their wedding beds, as their guests revel on.

In the morning, Siegfried and Kriemhild are radiant with their mutual love; while Gunther seems distraught and Brunhild distant and aloof. Gunther has none of the bridegroom's natural joy and pride. Indeed, that very afternoon, Gunther comes to confide in Siegfried and tell him of his humiliation. On their wedding night Brunhild tells Gunther that, although he has won her hand by his skill in the arena, she will not willingly give up her body to him. For to give herself to a man would break the spell of her warrior's strength, which she wishes to keep all her life. When Gunther tries by force to claim his nuptial rights, Brunhild merely laughs at him. She binds him up with her braided girdle and hangs him like a slaughtered pig from a peg on the wall until dawn. Once again Siegfried is drawn into an intrigue against the warrior-queen.

That night in darkness, using Tarnkappe, his magic cloak of invisibility, Siegfried enters Brunhild's room. In Gunther's place he lies in Brunhild's bridal bed. Thinking it is Gunther in the dark, Brunhild strikes Siegfried with such force that blood leaps from his mouth and he is thrown across the room. Wrestling with the hero, Brunhild grips Siegfried's hands so tightly that blood spurts from his nails and he is driven against the wall. Yet finally, Siegfried's huge strength prevails. He lifts her from the ground, throws her down upon the bed, and by main force crushes her in his gathered arms so fiercely that all the joints of her body crack at once. Only then does she submit and cry out to her conqueror to let her live.

Now most who tell this tale say that at this moment Siegfried is an honourable friend to Gunther and does not rest in the cradle of Brunhild's long limbs that night. But whatever the truth of the matter, in one way at least, Siegfried does dishonour this proud woman. For in the darkness, Siegfried sees the dull glint of red-gold. It is Brunhild's ring, and in his pride of conquest, he takes the ring from her hand. Then, as he leaves the marriage bed, he also takes the jewelled girdle of woven Nineveh silk as well.

In stealth, Siegfried flees the dark chamber, and Gunther comes to the bed of the vanquished bride who no longer dares to resist his advance. When the dawn comes, Brunhild is as pale and meek as the mildest bride. For with the loss of maidenhead and her ring, Brunhild's warrior strength flees her body forever. She becomes a submissive wife to King Gunther.

THE RIVAL QUEENS

Now 12 years pass happily. Siegfried and Kriemhild live and rule over the Netherlands and the Nibelungenland from their palace in Xanten, while Gunther and Brunhild live and rule over the Rhinelands. Then Gunther invites Siegfried and Kriemhild to come to a festival in his court.

Perhaps the ancient power of the ring is at work, or perhaps the fault is in Siegfried's pride. Whatever the reason, Siegfried makes a tragic error, for in Xanten he gives as a gift to Kriemhild the ring and the silken girdle he took from Brunhild in her wedding bed. And, even more foolishly, he reveals to Kriemhild the secret of winning the ring and the girdle.

So one day, the two queens meet at the cathedral door and a dispute arises among them as to who should enter first. Brunhild is rash and maintains that Kriemhild has displayed unwarranted arrogance toward her, for obviously Siegfried is nothing more than a vassal of Gunther.

Kriemhild will not stand for this insult. She argues that Siegfried is the greater man and no man's vassal. Filled with exasperation, Kriemhild's discretion is abandoned. To Brunhild, she holds up the stolen ring of red-gold, and then reveals the jewelled girdle of braided Nineveh silk that Brunhild once wore. Contemptuously, before all who

will listen, she claims that Brunhild had been Siegfried's concubine before she wed Gunther, and that Siegfried had taken these trophies after he had been the first to enjoy her body upon the bridal bed.

The humiliated Brunhild flees to Gunther with this tale and demands that her honour be redeemed. Full of anger, Gunther calls Siegfried to him. Alarmed at this scandalous talk, Siegfried tells Gunther that what his wife has said is untrue and that he had not so used Brunhild that night. With no gentleness, Siegfried chastises his wife, and demands that she apologize for this shameful argument. In his haste to make amends so that Brunhild should not discover the other stratagems by which he deceived and subdued her, Siegfried orders an iron ring of knights to form about him, and swears a sacred oath that all these tales are black lies.

This false oath is the final seal on Siegfried's fate. His honour is despoiled. For, although it seems that most accept this denial, the proof of the gold ring and the girdle cannot be withdrawn and rumour of the scandal of the marriage bed spreads. To Brunhild comes the steadfast Hagen of Troneck, the queen's champion and the king's stoutest vassal. Brunhild inflames Hagen's heart, and these two persuade Gunther that only blood vengeance can restore their honour.

SIEGFRIED'S DEATH

At this time rumours of war with the Danes arise once again in the Rhine. Siegfried once more makes ready for war, but Kriemhild has dire forebodings. Artfully, Hagen comes to Kriemhild, saying that he too has had evil omens concerning her husband but that he cannot believe these omens as all know that Siegfried is protected by the spell of dragon's blood. It is then that Kriemhild reveals the secret of Siegfried's mortality. For when Siegfried once bathed in dragon's blood, a lime leaf covered one place between his shoulder blades. In this place alone, Siegfried can be pierced with sharp steel. On Hagen's instructions, Kriemhild secretly sews a tiny cross on Siegfried's doublet over his one mortal place. Then Hagen swears he will always be at Siegfried's back, and will guard the hero from any unexpected blow.

The very next day, Hagen, Gunther and Siegfried go hunting in the royal forest. When Siegfried lies down to drink from a stream after a long chase, Hagen drives his spear into the cross and through Siegfried's back to his heart. Mortally wounded, Siegfried is like a wild, dying beast flailing the air. But, after Hagen strikes, Gunther seizes Siegfried's weapons and flees, so the hero might not wreak vengeance with his final breath. When at last Siegfried's life's blood spills out upon the forest floor and he breathes no more, the assassins return. They take up his body and carry it to the court, proclaiming that Siegfried has been treacherously murdered by lawless highwaymen.

With Siegfried's death, Brunhild believes her honour has been upheld by her husband Gunther and her champion Hagen. Not only has she brought death to the man who deceived her, but the proud rival queen who had humiliated her is now brought to despair. Further, because Kriemhild is without a husband, Gunther takes her under his protection, and by this pretext plunders her inheritance, the Nibelung treasure.

THE NIBELUNG TREASURE

In this treacherous way, the Burgundians make the Nibelung treasure their own. For days and nights an endless caravan of wagons filled with gold and jewels carries the vast treasure into the great walled city of Worms, where Gunther and Brunhild rule. This treasure entirely fills the city's greatest tower. Yet so rich is this hoard that King Gunther mistrusts its keepers and others who might steal it. Stealthily over the years, under the cover of night, Gunther and Hagen pillage all that huge treasure and take it to a secret place on the Rhine. There Gunther and Hagen find a deep river cavern and sink all that vast treasure of gold and gemstones, so only these two in all the world knows where it is hidden.

For a time the power and strength of Gunther's people are without parallel. With the Nibelung hoard in their possession, they are renowned as the wealthiest of nations. Indeed, because that famous treasure now rests in their land, the Burgundians of the Rhine soon become known by all people as the Nibelungs: possessors of the Nibelungen treasure; the luckiest of men.

Not all within the kingdom are content. The grieving Kriemhild for one is not deceived by the tale of Siegfried's death. She guesses well enough the truth of his murder. Gradually her despair is replaced by a desire for revenge. Daily she stares at the gold ring on her hand, which reminds her of the dispute that was the reason for her hero's treacherous murder.

KRIEMHILD AND ETZEL

At last Brunhild decides she can no longer have Kriemhild within the royal court, for she rightly fears that Siegfried's widow might ferment revolt. As chance would have it, Etzel the emperor of the Huns of the Danube has sent word to the Nibelung court. The noble and elderly ruler of the Huns wishes to make the fair Kriemhild his queen. He has often heard of her beauty, and further he would be honoured to marry and protect the widowed queen of Siegfried the Dragonslayer. To this proposal Gunther gives his blessing. He gives the hand of his sister to the emperor Etzel and sends her to the Hun city of Gram on the banks of the Danube. Now Gunther believes that he and Brunhild might live forever, secure from retribution for the slaying of Siegfried.

This is not to be. For although Kriemhild is taken to the mighty Huns' royal city of Gram and the palace of Etzel on the banks of the Danube, her desire for vengeance is never forgotten. Although the generous Etzel gives to her every luxury and she feigns happiness in his presence, Kriemhild works always toward one end.

The emperor Etzel is quite unaware of Kriemhild's intrigues and seems little concerned as his queen comes to command greater and greater power among the Huns. She gains the sworn allegiance and obedience of great numbers of Etzel's vassals. Many knights out of compassion, love or greed swear loyalty to Kriemhild above all others. After many years, when Kriemhild believes that her power is great enough, she persuades Etzel to invite all her kinsmen on a midsummer visit to the city of the Huns. So open-handed and fair has Etzel always been with the Nibelungs that they suspect no evil intent. So to Gram come the three Nibelung kings: Gunther, Gernot and Giselher; there also come the dauntless Hagen and his brother Dancwart; the mighty warriors Volker and Ortwine; and a thousand more heroic men as well. No nobleman is left within the walls of Worms, and from her tower Brunhild and her servants watch them go.

KRIEMHILD'S REVENGE

In the emperor's city the midsummer celebrations are filled with pageantry and pomp. There are tournaments, games and festivals of song and dance. Yet the Nibelungs do not take part in the celebrations, for Gunther and Hagen see the fierce light of hatred that is in Kriemhild's eyes. Well they know its source, although they had hoped she had long ago laid her hatred to rest. They realize they had received ill omens on their long journey to the land of the Huns.

On the twelfth day of the journey, they came to the wide banks of the Danube. There Hagen came upon the swan maidens, those fatal river women whom some call Nixies, and others call water sprites. From them Hagen won a prophetic vision: all the Nibelungs by fire and sword would perish, and none would live to return to the Rhinelands.

So, although all the Nibelungs had hoped that the Nixies had delivered to Hagen a false vision, the dreadful look of Kriemhild forewarns them of their doom. Thereafter, they go about fully armed among the revellers. They do not have long to wait. That very night Kriemhild acts while all the Nibelung knights sit in the feast hall. Secretly, without Etzel's knowledge, Kriemhild sends a force of armed men to the quarters of the Nibelung squires, and all those valiant youths are slaughtered. When news of the slayings reaches the feast hall, Hagen leaps to his feet at the feasting table. With relentless savagery, he draws his sword and strikes off the infant head of Ortlieb, Etzel's only child, as he plays upon his father's lap.

Then Hagen calls out to the Nibelungs, telling them they have fallen into a trap, that like the squires they too would all be slain. The Nibelung knights leap into battle and the hall becomes a slaughterhouse. Though Etzel and Kriemhild escape, two thousand Huns fall in that battle in the hall.

Much to Etzel's distress, Kriemhild urges on more of the Hunnish legions and allies. The feast hall is transformed: the tables are covered with severed limbs and heads, silver dishes are filled with human entrails, and gold cups brim with human blood. Kriemhild too is transformed; once the gentlest of women, she is now an avenging angel of death. Relentlessly, she urges the Huns into battle, and although more than half the Nibelungs have been slain, they hold the doors to the hall until a wall of bodies blocks the entrance, and the Huns have to clear their own dead to renew the fight.

Filled with fury, Kriemhild calls for torches and has the hall set ablaze to drive the Nibelungs into the open. But the fire does not drive the Nibelungs out, though many perish by flame, heat and smoke. They fight on through the blazing night. Taking refuge beneath the stone arches of the hall while the wooden structures burn about them, they battle on and drink the blood of the dead to slake their thirst.

Through the horror of that night a number of the Nibelungs survive, but with the dawn the queen calls forth many more grim Hunnish men-at-arms. These vengefully attack the Nibelungs in the burned wreckage of the feast hall. Yet these warriors find even the remnants of the Nibelung knights a terrible foe, and many fall before their pitiless weapons.

INTERVENTION OF DIETRICH

Some of the Nibelungs might yet have lived had not that mighty hero, Dietrich, the king of Verona, come to the aid of the Huns. Dietrich has no great desire to stand against the valiant Nibelungs; however, too many friends and kinsmen have now died at their hands. He knows he must act, so he sends his noble lieutenant Hildebrand with his men before him into the ruined hall. He asks Hildebrand to make some treaty between the Nibelungs and the Huns, so he himself need not be drawn into this feud.

But this act of reconciliation fails; the truce erupts at once in a bloody dispute that entirely eclipses both Dietrich's army and the ragged remainder of the Nibelungs. Only the wounded Hildebrand lives to return with the

Etzel the Emperor of the Huns

disastrous news. Grimly, Dietrich arms himself and comes to the ruined hall to find that only the exhausted but defiant Gunther and Hagen remain alive of all the Nibelungs. In a rage of despair, Dietrich uses his mighty strength to drive the exhausted Gunther and Hagen to the wall. It might have been the ghost of Siegfried himself that had come, so great is his might. The weapons of the Nibelungs – even the sword Balmung, which Hagen usurped – are struck from their hands, and they are subdued and bound by the fierce Dietrich.

Still, Dietrich is a man of compassion, for he implores Kriemhild to have pity on these brave knights. For a moment, it seems that Kriemhild will hold back her wrath. In truth, Kriemhild has now become an avenging fiend gone far beyond redemption. In the throne room she declares that there is yet the matter of her rightful inheritance to be resolved: the Nibelung treasure must be brought to Etzel's court.

THE DEATH OF KRIEMHILD

In secret, Kriemhild has already been to the cells. She meets Hagen and makes to him a false promise of freedom if he will tell her where the Nibelung treasure is hidden. Hagen is a dark and stoic man, and he trusts not a word that Kriemhild speaks. Hagen tells the queen he has sworn an oath never to reveal where the Nibelung treasure is buried while his lord, Gunther, lives.

Queen Kriemhild orders Hagen to be brought in chains to the throne room. Then, to the horror of all, Kriemhild throws the severed head of King Gunther – her own brother – upon the floor. The emperor Etzel and the hero Dietrich are aghast at the queen's savagery, but the fierce Hagen of Troneck defiantly laughs aloud.

There had been no oath of silence. Hagen had provoked the slaying because he feared that Gunther would trade his life for the treasure. But now that Gunther is gone, Hagen alone in all the world knows where that hoard is hidden, and no torture will ever make him tell. For if he cannot return the treasure to his queen, Brunhild, he can now at least deny that reward to her rival. Hagen laughs aloud, boasting that he would gladly suffer death and damnation to keep this last rich victory locked within his heart.

Hagen's defiance so enrages Queen Kriemhild that in an instant she takes into her hands Hagen's sword – the sword Balmung, which had once belonged to Siegfried. Then, before the emperor or his courtiers can recover from the first shock of the unnatural murder of Gunther, Kriemhild strikes off the head of Hagen of Troneck as well.

All now see the monstrous being that Kriemhild has become. At this last act of treachery, all the royal court recoil in horror. All know that no greater shame can befall a knight than to be slain by the hand of a woman. It is Dietrich's lieutenant, Hildebrand, who acts out the will of all the assembled nobles when he leaps forward with his drawn sword. In a deed that might almost have been merciful, he ends the tortured life of Queen Kriemhild with a single stroke.

With the death of Hagen, the last Nibelung lord is slain and the Nibelung treasure is gone forever from the sight of men. The Nixies and water sprites of the Rhine alone know where it lies, and they have no use for gold or gems. The ancient ring that was the cause of all this despair is

buried with Queen Kriemhild, who was once the gentlest of women; while her rival, Queen Brunhild, who was once the strongest of her sex, is now broken by the loss of husband, champion and all wealth. She mourns the disaster that has extinguished all her noble men-at-arms and left her alone in a ruined and empty realm.

So ends the tale of the rivalry of the two queens.

THE ORIGINS OF THE NIBELUNGENLIED

Although many of the German romances of hero cycles used elements of the Norse *Völsunga Saga*, the medieval epic the *Nibelungenlied* is the most direct rendering of that particular tale. Its hero Siegfried is definitely the Norse Sigurd the Dragonslayer. In part, the *Nibelungenlied* is an attempt by German royal houses to claim mythic ancestors in established heroic tradition; and in part it is authentic history. The heroic age for all the Teutonic (Germanic and Scandinavian) races of Northern Europe was the chaotic 5th and 6th centuries, when the authority of the Roman Empire was collapsing before the migrating Teuton tribes. The historical chieftains of those times became the subjects of oral traditions that elevated them to mythic status.

The events in the *Völsunga Saga* and the *Nibelungenlied* are both based on the historical events surrounding the catastrophic annihilation of the Burgundians in 436 CE by the Huns of Attila, who were acting as mercenary agents for the Roman Emperor. The *Nibelungenlied*, as we know it, was written by an anonymous poet around 1200 AD for performance in the Austrian court – or rather, he was the last poet to contribute to the *Nibelungenlied*, for the work

Opposite: War ravages and ruins the lands of the Nibelungs and the Huns

was the product of a heroic poetic tradition that began sometime in the 5th century.

PRINCESSES AND SHIELD MAIDENS

The characters of Brunhild and Kriemhild – and much of the plot for the *Nibelungenlied* and the *Völsunga Saga* – are also partly shaped by another historical character: the notorious Visigoth Queen Brunhilda. Born in about 540 CE, Brunhilda was married to King Sigebert of the Eastern Franks. King Sigebert's brother Chilperic was the king of the Western Franks and married Queen Brunhilda's sister. In the ensuing war between brothers, King Sigebert was murdered through intrigue in 575, and Brunhilda was made a captive. Her life was saved and her freedom won, however, by her captor's son, who took her as his wife. She soon became a powerful force

among the Franks, and over the 30 years of her influence she brought about the murders of no fewer than ten royal noblemen. Finally, in 613, a group of Frank noblemen decided to put an end to her intrigues. They tortured Brunhilda for three days, had her torn apart by wild horses, and then burned her on a pyre – an extraordinary and barbaric end to a remarkable historical character.

In *The Lord of the Rings*, the basic central plot of the *Nibelungenlied* can be found in an understated subplot involving the four-way romance of Aragorn–Arwen–Éowyn–Faramir. The shield maiden Éowyn of Rohan falls in love with Aragorn in the same hopeless way, it is implied, that the Amazonian warrior Queen Brunhild of Iceland falls for Siegfried. Siegfried is betrothed to the beautiful Kriemhild, in the same way that Aragorn is betrothed to beautiful Arwen of Rivendell. Tolkien's resolution of the love triangle in *The Lord of the Rings* is far happier and more gentlemanly, with none of the low trickery or bloody retribution of the *Nibelungenlied*.

CHANGING PERSPECTIVES

The *Nibelungenlied* displays many perspectives that sound strange to a modern reader. The *Nibelungenlied* epic is not primarily a vehicle for the hero Siegfried, as, say, the *Iliad* is for Achilles. It also appears that our sympathies with the valiant Siegfried in the first half are supposed to shift in the second half to the heroic deeds of his murderers, Hagen and Gunther. The epic is not even a history of a single dynasty or race. The Nibelungs are first one people, then another, then a third, depending on who controls the Nibelung treasure, which has become separated from the ring.

Opposite: Sigurd the Völsung discovers Brynhild the sleeping shield maiden

There are also other curiosities about the epic. In the *Völsunga Saga*, the historical Attila the Hun is Atli, a savage and treacherous tyrant. However, in the *Nibelungenlied*, the Hun king known as Etzel is portrayed as a humane and sympathetic character. This is certainly because of the politics of the Austrian court for whom the *Nibelungenlied* was composed.

Christian morality and chivalric traditions also resulted in changes. The extreme courtly behaviour of the knights and the coyness concerning the defloration of Brunhild is at odds with the straightforward Norse version. Also, there is undoubtedly a war-of-the-sexes aspect to the epic. Siegfried makes this clear in his battle with the Amazon. "If I now lose my life to this girl, the whole sex will become uppish and never obey their husbands forever after," he says. It does not seem to matter that Siegfried and Gunther cheat and lie to this obviously superior woman in the arena and in the bedroom. It all serves the higher moral purpose of keeping women subservient.

The warrior-maiden is also humbled and transformed – but more gently and without humiliation – in *The Lord of the Rings*. The shield maiden Éowyn who has slain the Witch-king is transformed by marriage into the gentle and subservient wife of Faramir, just as the unconquerable Amazon queen Brunhild is transformed by marriage into the gentle and subservient wife of Gunnar.

The double standard is also vividly demonstrated in the remarkable last scene of the *Nibelungenlied*. Here the narrator suggests that the proper and chivalric attitude of Queen Kriemhild toward Hagen – the knight who murdered her husband, stole her treasure and decapitated her only child – should have been mercy. When she demurs by cutting

Hagen's head off with Siegfried's sword, her behaviour is seen
as monstrous. In the chivalric tradition of the time, vengeance
is a male prerogative, and the slaying of even the vilest of
knights by a woman is unforgivable. Immediately, a knight
acts out the collective will of the court. He draws his own
sword and executes her.

In the *Nibelungenlied*, the ring is obviously separated from
the treasure before the tale properly begins. It is not with the
treasure, but on the hand of the Amazon queen. However,
one aspect of the ring is taken on in the treasure trove by the
Tarnkappe, the cloak of invisibility that Siegfried wins by
wrestling with the dwarf Alberich. (In the same way, the god
Loki wins the ring by wrestling with the dwarf Andvari, and
Frodo twice wrestles with Gollum for possession of the One
Ring.) The trick of invisibility that the One Ring possesses is
not present in Norse tales. In the *Nibelungenlied* Siegfried uses
the Tarnkappe for invisibility against the Amazon, while both
Bilbo and Frodo use the One Ring's invisibility against various
enemies, dragons and wraiths.

It is important also to point out that, even though the
treasure and the cape of invisibility take over aspects of the
ring's power, the ring remains the key to the epic's tragic
plot. It is the ring taken by Siegfried from Brunhild and
given to Kriemhild that ultimately seals the fate of all in the
Nibelungenlied, just as surely as the movement of the One
Ring seals the fate of all in *The Lord of the Rings*.

PART

TEN

GREEK
AND ROMAN
MYTHS

There is one ancient Greek myth that tells of the forging of the first ring. The tale begins at the dawn of time, long before humans or even gods existed. In fact, the story of the first ring is bound up with the tale of the coming of the gods and the creation of man.

The Titans were the first race to rule the primeval world. They were the giant sons and daughters of Gaea, who is Mother Earth. Titans were as tall as the hills and both wise and strong. They also possessed magic powers with which they brought forth unlimited wealth and bounty.

The Titans gave birth to many children: sons and daughters who became the spirits of rivers and forests. All nature was animated by their offspring: the nymphs of the sea, the mermaids, the naiads, the satyrs and the sylphs.

THE WAR OF THE TITANS AND OLYMPIAN GODS

One of the wisest of the Titans was gifted with the art of prophecy, and for this reason was named Prometheus, which means "foresight". By this gift Prometheus had foreknowledge of the end of this age. He saw that by craft and cunning the Titans would be overthrown by the lesser race of the gods. Furthermore, he knew that his own fate was to be different from that of his soon-to-be-vanquished race; that it was to be bound up with that of these youthful gods.

When the war between the Titans and the gods was fought, it all but consumed the world. For ten long years the terror of that war racked the earth. From the height of Olympus, Zeus, the storm god, hurled down his thunderbolts; while his brother Poseidon, the sea god, with his trident commanded the earth to quake. Yet with their strength and

Opposite: Yavanna and Aulë look over their creations

magicians' powers, the Titans stood and fought the gods with glittering armour and shining spears. But valiant though they were, the Titans were overwhelmed by the gods. They were blasted by thunderbolts and the earth was rent from under them, causing them to fall into the deep pits of Tartarus, over which cruel Hades, the god of the underworld, ruled, and from which none could escape.

PROMETHEUS AND THE CREATION OF MEN

The Titan Prometheus was not condemned to such a fate as his brother, Atlas, who eternally held the weight of the heavens on his shoulders. Prometheus had taken no part in the war against the gods, and though he grieved for his kin, he long had known their fate. Instead, he went among the new gods and gave these harsh new rulers gifts of wisdom and knowledge. Prometheus turned his hand more and more to the arts of shaping metals and the substances of the earth he loved.

He chose as a companion the lame son of Zeus named Hephaestus, the least haughty and overbearing of the gods. To Hephaestus he brought the fire and the forge, and with that god shared his deep knowledge of the earth. In the volcanic hearts of mountains, Prometheus taught Hephaestus the skills of the forging of metals. There they forged jewelled crowns, sceptres and golden thrones for the gods of Olympus. They made bright weapons and armour blessed with magical powers. Hephaestus the Smith soon became so valued by Zeus that he gave the lame god the hand of Aphrodite, the beautiful goddess of love, in marriage.

Opposite: The light of the first sunrise brings about the miracle of the Awakening of Men upon Middle-earth

Yet far-seeing Prometheus had also employed other crafts in his delving and forging. For the skills of the magician as well as the smith were endowed to those of the Titan race, so that in time the secret of life itself came to him. And, as is well known, Prometheus was the deity who shaped men from clay and breathed into them the breath of life. Furthermore, it was Prometheus who brought to men the gift of fire, for in their beginning they lived in darkness. With this gift of fire came also the light of wisdom and the heat of unquenchable desire, and all the things that make men greater than beasts and cause them to strive to achieve immortal fame.

THE PUNISHMENT OF PROMETHEUS

◆

The Olympian gods were greatly displeased, for they wished no rivals in the world, and claimed that Prometheus had given to the mortals what the gods alone should possess. Yet the act could not be undone and the fire could not be quenched. In wrath, Zeus commanded Hephaestus to forge a great chain of unbreakable adamantine, the iron of the gods. Then he commanded that Prometheus be taken into the Asian wilderness among the White Mountains, between Scythia and Cimmeria, and upon the mountain called the Caucasus be chained. To that rock, Zeus swore Prometheus would forever be bound. To Prometheus Zeus sent a great eagle and a vulture of immense size. By these cruel birds, Prometheus's side was pierced and his liver torn out. Each night his liver grew again, only to be torn from him the next day. To him also came the fiery sun and the freezing rain and hail. Thus, like his brethren beneath the earth, Prometheus was filled with eternal pain.

Yet Prometheus endured and did not repent his deeds.
By night came many nymphs, sylphs and spirits who grieved
for him and sang soothing songs. Even some few of the race
of men dared come to that terrible wilderness and seek his
counsel. Yet none had the strength to break his bonds, and he
seemed forever doomed to this torture.

As the long ages passed, it is said that the gods became
less cruel, and though their treatment of men was not always
fair or good, they came to favour many among that mortal
race and even love them. Between gods and men there grew a
bond and a union, and from that union came many offspring.
Mightiest of all of these was Heracles, the son of Zeus.

Zeus had come at last to regret his punishment of
Prometheus. However, he was restrained by his own
unbreakable oath of eternal bondage. However, when
Heracles went into the Asian wilderness, Zeus did not drive
him away from the White Mountains, and allowed him to
seek out Prometheus. Zeus knew that only Heracles possessed
the strength to break the chains of adamantine, and the
courage to slay the eagle and the vulture.

PROMETHEUS AND ANNATAR — LORDS OF GIFTS

When Prometheus was at last freed, Zeus spoke to him in
a voice of thunder. Zeus swore that he would keep his oath
of bondage, yet allow Prometheus to keep his freedom. So
Zeus took from the chain of adamantine a broken link, and
from Mount Caucasus he took a fragment of rock. With his
immortal hand, Zeus welded the stone to the link. He then
took the hand of Prometheus, and about his finger he closed
the link of adamantine. By this device Zeus kept his oath to

Next page: Great Eagles – the emissaries of Zeus, King
of the Greek gods

chain the Titan to the rock of Caucasus for ever, and yet he fulfilled his promise to let Prometheus walk free.

This was how the first ring was made.

Afterward, it is said, men came to wear rings to honour Prometheus, the bringer of fire and the father of man. It is claimed that the ring is a sign of both the smith who is master of fire and the magician who is master of life. And those who are kings of men wear the ring as a sign of their descent from Prometheus and the Titans who once ruled the earth.

In Prometheus, the good Titan who brought life and fire to the human race, we have a mirror opposite to Tolkien's Sauron, the evil sorcerer who brought death and darkness. However, when Sauron appeared in the Second Age in disguise among the Elven-smiths of Eregion as the mysterious stranger Annatar the Lord of Gifts, he must have seemed everything to the Elves that Prometheus was to humans. For Annatar the Lord of Gifts was also a magician-smith who, like Prometheus, defied the gods by giving away forbidden gifts of knowledge and skill. With Annatar's guidance, Celebrimbor and the Elven-smiths of Ostin-Edhil in Eregion learned secrets of the smith and the magician matched only by the Valar themselves. Only after Annatar tricked the Elves into forging the Rings of Power did they learn the terrible price of Annatar's gifts. The price demanded of Prometheus's gifts was that the Titan himself be eternally bound and enslaved. The price demanded of Sauron's gifts was that the Elves be eternally bound and enslaved.

The Greek legend of the first ring links the ring to many primal images of power, which later emerge in the ring quest tradition and are linked with alchemy and metallurgy. In this tale, the first ring is solidly connected with the powers of the magician and the smith. Curiously, Prometheus, the father of man, the giver of fire and the master of smiths, has a ring forged of iron in the Caucasian Mountains: the very place where the secret of iron-smelting was discovered.

PART
ELEVEN

JUDEO-
CHRISTIAN
LEGENDS

The contribution of Judeo–Christian tradition to Tolkien's imaginative writing is both paradoxical and – in one particular legend – profound. In many respects, the early Judeo–Christian world is very unlike Tolkien's world. Tolkien purposely created a world that is without formal religion. Although Tolkien's characters do not quite worship the Valar, their beliefs are very much closer to the pantheism of the pagan Teutons, Celts and Greeks than they are to the fierce monotheism of the Old Testament Hebrews.

However, in Tolkien's tales of creation of his world of Arda in *The Silmarillion* and subsequent books, we see biblical language and themes that add an undeniable grandeur to the event. In these tales, we also see that, behind the multiplicity of appearance, Tolkien conceived a primal cause in the form of a single entity, which is not far removed from the Judeo–Christian monotheistic God.

ILÚVATAR AND MELKOR

A clear example of Judeo–Christian influences can be seen in Tolkien's Eru the One – whom the Elves call Ilúvatar. Through him all things entered the great void of space. In the beginning these were his "thoughts" in the form of the Ainur, or "Holy Ones". These vastly powerful Ainur spirits were given life and independent powers, and in the Timeless Halls Ilúvatar commanded them to sing in a celestial choir. This is known as the Music of the World, out of which all things came.

Religious overtones such as these continue when Melkor, the most powerful of the mighty Ainur spirits, being the lord of darkness, saw things differently. This resulted in his disruption of the celestial music, and ultimately a war of

Opposite: Illuin, one of the two Lamps, that brought light to the Isle of Almarin, the first kingdom of the Valar within the spheres of the world

powers in the heavens, which is later transferred to a war of powers on earth.

Once the Ainur spirits enter Arda, they are transformed and become the Valar who strongly resemble the early pagan gods of Olympus and Asgard. However, in their early celestial manifestations, the Ainur are very like powerful Judeo–Christian angels and archangels. Certainly the grand conflict that arises between the Eru and Melkor owes much to the war between God and his rebel angel, Satan, as portrayed in John Milton's *Paradise Lost*. Melkor's revolt both in its celestial form and within the spheres of the world greatly resembles the cataclysmic War in Heaven, when Satan led his rebel angels against the angels of God.

In character and deeds, Melkor is very like John Milton's Satan, who is destroyed by pride and ultimately damned. His is very much a case of one who, like Milton's Satan, would rather "reign in Hell, than serve in Heaven".

Melkor the Lord of Darkness, and his eventual successor, Sauron the Dark Lord, make war on Ilúvatar by proxy within the spheres of the world. Their grudge with Ilúvatar drives them on to destroy and corrupt all that He has created. This is the basis for all conflict on Tolkien's Middle-earth and results in a morality of absolute good and evil.

HEBREWS AND ELVES — CHOSEN PEOPLES

❖

Many other Hebrew heroes and leaders were associated with rings of supreme authority or power. In the Middle Ages, Moses, who led the exodus of the Hebrews out of Egypt back to the promised land of Israel, was commonly associated with the use of magic rings.

Previous Page: Melkor and Ungoliant in Valinor

Aside from this, Tolkien draws further biblical parallels in *The Silmarillion* between his Elves and the Hebrew tribes of Moses. Like Moses' people, the Elves are a "chosen people" who endure terrible hardships of mass migration to a "Promised Land". The "Great Journey" of the Elves across the wildernesses of Middle-earth is to Eldamar, the promised homeland of the Elves in the Undying Lands – just as the Hebrews come to Israel, the promised homeland of the Jews. Both are comparable in that they are divinely summoned: the Elves by the Valar Manwë; the Hebrews by the god Jehovah.

Much later, Tolkien describes a second migration of the Noldor Elves back to Middle-earth, which is also reminiscent of the Hebrew exodus. However, it differs in that the Hebrews' leader, Moses, acted at the command of his god, Jehovah, while the Elves' charismatic leader, Fëanor, acted *against* the command of the Valar Manwë.

BIBLICAL RINGS OF POWER

Beyond the philosophical comparisons, however, the strongest links between biblical legends and Tolkien's tales relate to beliefs in the power of rings. By biblical times, all kingdoms and nations had long accepted the tradition of the ring as a symbol of a monarch's authority. The king's ring not only marked him as the monarch, but the ring could be said to possess power in itself. Often, in the absence of the king, the ring or the ring's seal could be used to carry the full authority of the ruler. In such a way, the king might make a proclamation over all his lands, or delegate authority to his servants and subjects.

These rings of authority were made in many forms. Most often they were signet rings inscribed or marked with the symbol and name of their master on fixed seals of stone, crystal, amber or even hard gems. These could then make the mark of the king's seal with ink, or on wax or clay. Assyrian monarchs wore rings with engraved cylinder seals set in roller bezels. Some carried no marking at all, but in some such cases the properties of the sacred stone or precious metal carried their authority.

The pharaohs of Egypt wore the great scarab ring of ebony stone inlaid with gold. The scarab was set on a swivel bezel so it might be turned to reveal the cartouche: the great seal of the pharaoh. Control of the ring brought control of Egypt, for the seal was the word of the pharaoh, and the word of the pharaoh was sacred law.

KING SOLOMON'S RING

◆

The most famous ring legend in the Judeo–Christian tradition is the one linked with King Solomon. Tradition tells us that Solomon was not only considered a powerful king and wise man, but he was also believed to be the most powerful magician of his age. These magician's powers were attributed largely to his possession of a magic ring. The legend of "King Solomon's Ring" is certainly the one tale of the Judeo–Christian tradition that had the most profound influence on the imagination of Tolkien in his composition of *The Lord of the Rings*.

There can be little doubt that Tolkien was familiar with this ancient biblical tale of a sorcerer-king who (like Sauron) used a magic ring to command all the demons of the earth, and bent them to the purpose of ruling his empire. Just as Solomon uses his magic ring to build his great temple on Moriah, so Sauron uses the One Ring to build his great tower in Mordor. Of all rings of myth and legend, Solomon's Ring most resembles the One Ring of *The Lord of the Rings*.

Solomon's Ring is also like Sauron's One Ring in that its power can corrupt its master, even one as wise as Solomon. In the figure of the demon Asmodeus we see the subtle agent of evil who corrupts the wise but fatally proud King Solomon of Israel, and through possession of the ring causes his downfall. In the figure of the demon Sauron we see the subtle agent of evil who corrupts the wise but fatally proud King Ar-Pharazôn of Númenor, and through possession of the ring causes his downfall.

Curiously, the tale of Solomon's Ring also has elements that invite comparison with that other miraculous quest

Opposite: Earendil the Mariner with the Silmaril on his brow in his celestial form as the Morning Star

object of Tolkien's mythology. Just as the Elven King Thingol succeeds in acquiring the brilliant, light-radiating jewel called the Silmaril, so the Hebrew King Solomon succeeds in acquiring the brilliant, light-radiating jewel called the Schamir. Both are heirlooms of their races: the Silmaril was once the sacred jewel of the ancestral leader of the Elves, Fëanor; while the Schamir was the sacred jewel of the ancestral leader of the Jews, Moses. In Tolkien, the Silmaril is finally set into a gold headband and shines from the brow of the celestial traveller, Eärendil the Mariner, in the form of the Morning Star. Once the Schamir is returned to the Hebrews, the radiant jewel appears to fit perfectly on the golden bezel of Solomon's Ring. The jewel doubles the power of Solomon's Ring and illuminates the "One Name" of God.

THE GIFT OF THE RING

The story of how the ring came to Solomon is bound up with the tale of the building of the Temple of Yahweh, the Lord God Almighty. Solomon had set the slaves of Israel and the craftsmen of Tyre to work on the wondrous Temple of Mount Moriah, but Yahweh had forbidden the use of iron in its construction. Although a great multitude strove to build the Temple, its growth was slow. The slaves and craftsmen laboured longer and longer each month, but it was as if nothing was accomplished and each day the king's builders grew paler and thinner. At last one named Jair, who was a master builder and Solomon's favourite slave, came to him. Once young and vigorous, Jair was now shrunken and utterly emaciated. Each night, he claimed, a vampire came and sucked his blood and the

Opposite: King Solomon enthralled and corrupted by the demon Asmodeus

blood of his workmen. And the same demon spirited away food and gold, and materials of marble, cedar and stone.

Deeply troubled, Solomon climbed to a high jutting rock on Mount Moriah and prayed unto Yahweh. Suddenly the emerald-winged archangel Michael, in a vision of brilliant light, appeared before him bearing a gold ring and said: "Take, O Solomon, King, son of David, the gift which the Lord God, the highest Zebaot, hath sent unto thee. With it thou shalt lock up all the demons of the earth, male and female; and with their help thou shalt build up Jerusalem. But thou must wear this seal of God." Solomon was amazed but took into his hands the ring which was small and of pure gold. On the bezel of the ring was the seal of God: the five-pointed star of the pentalpha and the four letters of the name of Yahweh (YHWH). This was the ring from beneath the throne of God, which some claimed had been Adam's before the Fall of Man, and others claimed was Lucifer's before the expulsion of the rebel angels.

Standing alone on Mount Moriah, Solomon slid the ring onto his finger and suddenly he was filled with the sound of a great music. It was the music of the many spheres of the universe in the symphony of their turning. He was possessed now of an understanding of life and beauty beyond the grasp of other mortals. By the power of the ring he understood the language of the birds, animals and fish. He could talk with the trees and herbs and knew the deep secrets of earth and stone. Within the world nothing was hidden from him.

BEELZEBUL, LORD OF DEMONS

Armed with the ring, Solomon now dared to employ its greatest powers and summoned the vampire Ornias, who had weakened Jair and frustrated the building of the Temple. He told Ornias that he must compensate him by cutting stones by day for the Temple, and Ornias bowed low and obeyed the command of the ring lord. But first Solomon asked Ornias, "Who is the lord of all the demons?" Ornias answered, "Beelzebul". Solomon gave Ornias the ring and told him to summon Beelzebul to his presence. Ornias took it, went to Beelzebul and said, "Hither, Solomon calls thee." And Beelzebul laughed and said, "Who is this Solomon?" Then Ornias threw the ring at Beelzebul's breast, saying: "Solomon the King summons you under the seal of Yahweh." Beelzebul cried aloud with a mighty voice, emitted a great flame and came into Solomon's presence.

So did Beelzebul, proud lord of the demons, bow low before the feet of the master of the ring and await his pleasure. At Solomon's command Beelzebul summoned all the demons of the earth before the king. Never had so many great spirits been gathered at the command of a mortal. There were demons of two kinds: the common demons of the mortal earth, who are the spirits of disease; and the sons of Heaven, fallen.

In the first group were the thirty-six Decani, the genii of sickness for every part of the body, and the seven who in the shape of stars cause moral sickness. All of these were deformed and ghastly. Upon them Solomon set his seal and they fell afflicted with their own maladies. Then he imprisoned them in copper cylinders. Some say that no man fell sick until the Temple was finished; others that there was no more sickness until the Chaldeans sacked the Temple, opened the bottles in ignorance, and inflicted sickness once more upon the world.

In the second group were the fallen angels in many forms. There was Rabdos, who travelled the earth in a dog's likeness and always had a dog's head. There was the Pterodrakon and the three-headed dragon. There was Envy, who had the limbs of man and no head, and in consequence ate people's minds in his search for a head. There were the three Liliths, beautiful enchantresses: Onoskelis the fair-skinned and naked; Enepsigos the winged; and Obyzuth the serpent-tailed; together with the hermaphroditic Akephalos, who had eyes for nipples. There was Epiphas the great wind, Kunopeigos the lord of

the Red Sea, Lix Terrax the Sandstorm; and many others of changed or combined shapes: asses' ears above the manes of lions; elephants' trunks under the wings of bats; vultures' talons in the scales of fish; toothed feet; headed arms; and some composed all of entrails and organs. And though Beelzebul was their lord, he was not Solomon's chief adversary among all the demons. This was the great Asmodeus: tall, mocking, sardonic and handsome, albeit bat-winged and cloven-footed.

ASMODEUS AND THE SCHAMIR

Before this terrible host Solomon raised his hand adorned with the gold ring, and he commanded them all to work upon the Temple of Yahweh. Those who rebelled were shut under the great seal into jars, like the demons of disease. So at this time Solomon used the power of the ring only to achieve the work of Yahweh, and all went well with him and his kingdom. But still, because of God's prohibition of iron, the building went slowly, for the cutting of the great stones of the Temple was long and difficult work.

Solomon held counsel with his wise men, and the scholars among them told him of that brilliant and magical gem called the Schamir, which Moses had used to engrave the names of the tribes of Israel upon the precious stones of the high priest's ephod (apron). They claimed that the power of this gem was so great it could cut any substance. But neither the scholars nor the demons could tell Solomon where the Schamir could be found. Only Asmodeus possessed this knowledge, and during Solomon's absence he had escaped. Yet Solomon pursued and trapped him, and with the ring forced him to reveal where the Schamir might be found. Asmodeus said that the Schamir had been entrusted to the Angel of the Sea after Moses' death, and that it was now under the protection of the Sea Eagle. Solomon searched out the nest of this gigantic and deathless bird and laid a dome of crystal over it. When the Sea Eagle came and could not reach her young, she flew off and returned with the Schamir. She placed it on the crystal, which instantly shattered. The slaves of Solomon appeared and cast spears and bolts of iron at the Sea Eagle. In fright she fled and the slaves retrieved the magical gem that could cut rock like butter.

The Schamir fitted exactly upon the bezel of Solomon's gold ring. Through it the pentalpha and the One Name could be seen, shimmering and pulsating with such colour and radiance that some have claimed that the ring was also set with diamond, sapphire, emerald and ruby. But in truth there was only one gem, and by its power the rock of the temple was cut.

Yahweh spoke in the night to Solomon, warning him that the power of his ring was now doubled. He told Solomon that he must no longer ignore Michael's first instruction to wear the ring at all times. It would preserve him from harm and keep him on the throne.

SOLOMON AND NAAMAH

After the finding of the Schamir, Asmodeus was kept under bonds by Solomon in his palace. And from him the king learned many secrets of the future, for the fallen sons of Heaven – who are the stars of the zodiac – eavesdrop at the gates of Heaven, and hear the plans of Yahweh and his angels. But Solomon underestimated Asmodeus, who had never told him the full truth about God's workings, but instead lulled him into a false security. Moreover, with the Temple finished, Solomon paid more attention to pleasure than to piety; and Yahweh would not be mocked.

One day Asmodeus enraptured the king with a tale of the power and visions of the demons. Solomon asked how they could be so happy and gifted if a mere mortal like himself could keep their greatest prince under bonds. Asmodeus answered that Solomon had only to loosen his fetter and lend him the ring, and he would prove his power and ecstatic vision. Solomon agreed. Asmodeus took the ring and placed it on his hand. By its doubled power the demon rose like a mountain before Solomon until one wing touched Heaven and the other touched the earth. He snatched up Solomon and hurled him out of Israel into the vast wilderness of the south.

Some legends say that Asmodeus then passed himself off as the king, but the authoritative version reveals that he conjured up a counterfeit Solomon who appeared in every way like the king (though some of his wives and concubines were puzzled and troubled by their lord's strange new appetites). Asmodeus himself flew out of Israel and returned to the freedom of his mountain fastness, hurling the ring into the depths of the Red Sea.

For three years Solomon wandered, an unrecognized beggar, atoning for his sins, while a counterfeit king sat on the throne. He came to the city of Ammon, took service as a kitchen skivvy in the palace of its king, and proved so talented that he was made chief cook. The king's daughter, Naamah, fell in love with Solomon, and the Ammonite king, outraged, had the lovers taken to the desert to starve.

But Solomon still knew the language of the wild things, and by his wisdom he and Naamah found enough food and water to survive until they came to the sea. There, Solomon helped a fisherman draw in his nets to the shore and he was rewarded with a fish. When Naamah cleaned the fish she found a ring in its belly – the ring that Asmodeus had cast into the sea. Solomon put on the ring, gave thanks to Yahweh, and transported himself and Naamah to Jerusalem in a trice. The counterfeit Solomon fell before the true king and vanished under the ring's seal.

THE CORRUPTION OF SOLOMON

The true Solomon was restored to his kingdom and his great wealth. Yet as time passed, Solomon became once again corrupted. He grew lustful and hedonistic, and thus fell from grace with Yahweh. He began sacrificing to the gods of his various wives as well as to the Hebrew God. Above all, he was besotted with his Jebusite queen and used his ring to build her goddess, Ashtaroth, a great temple and idol on the slopes of Mount Moriah.

Then, Asmodeus, who was his evil tempter in all this, brought word from his eavesdropping at Heaven's gate that the kingdom would be split at Solomon's death; that the Temple and his books would be destroyed, and that the demons of disease would be released again.

Solomon repented, but it was too late and Asmodeus's prophecies came about. However, it is said that Solomon died upright, leaning on his staff, and that the demons continued to work on his plans for many years after, not knowing that he was dead and that the power of the ring was now unmanned. At length, a snake curled about the staff and it snapped, and then the demons scattered.

The ring is thought to have been placed in the Holy of Holies in the Ark of the Covenant itself, and never captured. A later magician went to rescue it when the soldiers of Titus were destroying the Temple. He saw it and touched it, but then fainted and was carried to a strange land where a voice told him that the ring had been taken back to Heaven.

PART

TWELVE

EASTERN MYTHOLOGY

The epic hero of the Far East, Geser, was a warrior, magician, smith and king who ruled the greatest kingdom in the East. He is capable of many feats of heroism and magic. His confirmation as king comes when the supernatural guardians of the kingdom allow him entry into a crystal mountain where great treasures are kept.

As the king, Geser takes possession of these great and countless treasures. Without doubt, the most important is the emblematic throne of the realm, on which rests a huge, gold mandala ring that is known as the "life" of the land, with a crystal vessel at its centre, from which flows the shining "waters of immortality".

GESER AND KURKAR

Geser's early life was not an easy one. Although born a royal prince, while he is still a child his parents are slain by Kurkar, the evil sorcerer and ruler of a large mountain kingdom. The orphaned Geser is found in a heap of rubbish and adopted by a poor smith, who raises him as an apprentice. Under the adopted name of Chori, he survives many attempts by sorcerers to kill him. He becomes an extraordinary alchemist by combining his skills as a smith with his inherited powers of sorcery. He creates many wonders in his smithy for his master, but for himself he forges an unbreakable sword from celestial (meteoric) iron.

Geser prepares himself for his ultimate duel with his great enemy, Kurkar. However, he knows that his enemy cannot be slain until a huge iron mandala ring or talisman that is kept in the palace treasury is destroyed. This huge iron talisman contains the "life" or "soul" of Kurkar and all his ancestors.

Opposite: Mountain Kingdom of
Kurkar the Evil Sorcerer

This sacred iron had been venerated for many centuries and in it reposed the vital essence of the dynasty. The evil Kurkar himself says: "It is the 'life' of my ancestors. Sometimes sounds come from it, at other times it speaks."

Geser tricks Kurkar into allowing him access to the iron talisman. However, it is believed Kurkar is safe because the iron cannot be melted or forged by any known means. The fire of the furnace does not even redden the sacred iron. Geser is warned by the master smith: "It is folly to think that it will let itself be forged."

Geser, however, is no ordinary smith and accepts the challenge. He summons his supernatural brothers and a multitude of spirits who manage to build a huge furnace and fill it with "coal piled high as mountains". This results in an inferno that is sufficient to forge the iron mandala. Geser and his supernatural brothers strike the iron mandala with hammer blows that sound like thunder. At last the iron "life" of Kurkar and his ancestors is broken, and we are told "the three worlds shook" with its destruction.

Once this is achieved, Geser puts on his glittering armour and takes up his sword of celestial iron. In all his shining glory, Geser appears before the evil Kurkar. Geser declares his true identity to him and his mission of vengeance. Then, with a single stroke, Geser cuts off the sorcerer's head.

Opposite: the Talisman

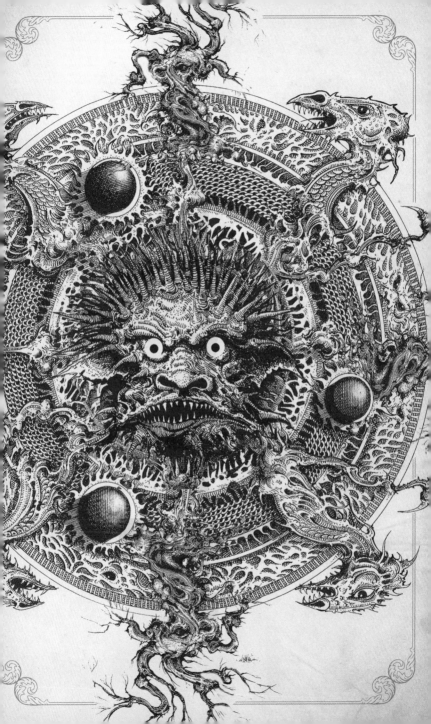

GESER, KURKAR AND SAURON

In Tolkien's *The Lord of the Rings*, the evil Sauron shares many characteristics with Geser and Kurkar. Like Geser, Sauron is both a supernaturally gifted smith capable of creating unmatched wonders upon his forge, and a magician capable of terrifying acts of sorcery. Both have mountain strongholds, and both must keep safe the golden rings by whose powers they rule their kingdoms.

At this point the comparison between Geser and Sauron largely ceases. Geser becomes an avenging angel of light, while Sauron the Dark Lord is much more closely allied to the values of the evil Kurkar. Kurkar – like both Geser and Sauron – also has a ring or talisman that must be kept safe and by whose power he rules his kingdom. However, Kurkar's iron talisman is much more like Sauron's One Ring because both are inherently evil, and the sorcerers' lives depend on the survival of the ring. Kurkar's talisman also shares the One Ring's characteristic of being almost indestructible. Normal fires do not even cause the metal in them to redden. Both require supernatural fires of volcanic intensity to melt them down.

The destruction of Kurkar's iron ring in Geser's volcanic forge-room causes a cataclysm in which "the three worlds shook". This is matched by the climax of *The Lord of the Rings*, when the destruction of Sauron's One Ring in Mount Doom's volcanic forge-room causes a comparable cataclysm in which "the earth shook, the plain heaved and cracked, and … the skies burst into thunder seared with lightning."

ALCHEMICAL ROOTS

◆

The Eastern epic of Geser – with its gold and iron mandala rings – is very obviously rooted in the ancient alchemical traditions. As touched upon earlier in this book, Alchemy combined the knowledge of the smith/smelter/miner with the supernatural powers of the magician/sorcerer/shaman. Geser is a warrior-king who is both a smith and a magician. To such a hero, all things are possible. He assumes many forms, creates invulnerable weapons, conjures up phantom armies, and creates wealth and prosperity for his people.

In Asian myth and history, the connection between alchemy or metallurgy and the power of kings and heroes is often more obviously stated than it is in Europe. Perhaps this is because eastern religions or philosophies are not in conflict with their shamanistic and alchemical traditions. Nor do they appear to have Christianity's need to vilify or eliminate these traditions.

Tradition insists, for instance, that the great historic Mongol conqueror Genghis Khan was descended from a family of smiths. So too was the legendary Tartar hero Kok Chan, who possessed a ring that – like Sauron's One Ring – hugely increased his already formidable powers. Legends telling of heroes or villains possessing external souls that are kept hidden within objects outside the body are found in many cultures throughout the world. The legends spring from a number of sources. However, when the soul is kept in a metal object or a ring, one can be certain that the source of the legend is the magician-smith tradition of alchemy.

The epic events of Geser's life demonstrate the ancient alchemical belief that not only can individual souls or lives be kept in a ring or talisman, but so can the souls or lives of

Next page: The defeat and surrender of the Shang Empire

entire dynasties and whole nations. This certainly parallels Tolkien's epic adventure, where Sauron the Dark Lord's entire evil empire collapses with the One Ring's destruction.

CHINA — RINGS OF JADE

The ancient histories of China tell how the monarchs of China wore rings that were unlike the rings of the West. For the alchemists of China believed that jade was the purest and most sacred substance, and the greatest value was placed on it. Their ruler's ring was not of gold or of some gem, but was a simple stone ring made from a unique blue jade. This was the sign of the power and glory of those omnipotent emperors through nearly four thousand years.

This blue jade ring was known as the Sky Ring of the Shang Dynasty, and the fate of this ring was bound up with the fate of China. There is one ancient tale concerning one of the emperors who failed to uphold its tradition and suffered through the curse of the ring.

Zhou Xin was the 30th and last of the Shang emperors. He was corrupt, greedy, cruel and foolish; and he should not rightly have had the throne. He abused his power. He indulged only in pleasure and ostentation, and he did not possess the one true ring of blue jade called the Sky Ring of Shang.

Zhou Xin's father, the emperor Di Yi, had an older son called Weiziqi, who was born when the empress was still his favourite concubine. Weiziqi was modest, learned and pious. His father named him his heir and, in a secret ceremony on his deathbed, handed him the Sky Ring of blue jade that was the sacred sign of the Shangs.

But on the emperor Di Yi's death, the ambitious Zhou Xin claimed that his brother Weiziqi had no right to the throne, being born out of wedlock, and Zhou usurped him. Thereafter Zhou Xin ruled the empire, but was always bitterly jealous of Weiziqi and plotted against him. Weiziqi retired to his estates in Wei, and some power protected him from all attempts on his life and property.

ZHOU XIN AND DAJI

But with the rule of Zhou Xin, a great imbalance came to the empire. The ceremonies of the ring were abolished; the wisdom of the Sky ring was lost. Zhou oppressed his people and gathered to himself great wealth while enjoying many decadent and hedonistic pleasures.

It is said Zhou Xin had concubines beyond number, but he always desired more. On hearing of the beauty of Daji, a princess of a neighbouring kingdom, he did not hesitate to demand her. When he was refused, he led his people into a bloody and disastrous war. At great price he won the pearl of that blameless kingdom, and with cruel torture he put to death Daji's father, mother and brothers.

The cruel Zhou Xin found this woman to be fair indeed. Her face was as the white full moon and her beauty outshone that of Zhou's other concubines, as the moon outshines the stars. He proclaimed her the most beautiful woman in the world, but some believed that the lovely Daji had bewitched the emperor so that she might find some way to avenge the slaughter of her family.

Although the people of the empire had already suffered grievously in war because of the charms of this princess, Zhou Xin commanded that they must build a palace befitting her beauty. This was to be the Deer Tower (the Luhtae), the greatest building in the world. It stood like a sheer mountain looming above the city of Po. To this vain purpose, Zhou Xin enslaved all his people for seven long years and impoverished the nation. Neglecting all other duties of his high office, he allowed the land to fall into ruin. There was famine and plague, and Zhou Xin even failed to maintain the power of the armies that had allowed the Shangs to dwell in peace for so long.

THE FINAL BETRAYAL

On the borders of the empire, the warlord Wan Wang, the duke of Zhou, looked upon the Shang lands with concern and dismay. Troubled by what he saw, he consulted the oracles of bone for divine guidance. He raised an army of chariots, cavalry and foot-soldiers, and, after receiving a favourable sign from the oracles, he went to war. With great ceremony Wan Wang crossed the Huang River and entered into the empire of the Shangs unchallenged.

Now Zhou Xin betrayed his people for the last time. He had the keeper of the treasury bring all that remained in the vaults of the nation and all the ancient Imperial Jades of the Shangs to him. Then he climbed to the top of the Deer Tower and set fire to himself and all the wealth of the empire. His people were left with nothing, and all their labour of seven years was destroyed.

Wan Wang observed the ceremonies of the time. Thus, as conqueror, he rode to the ruins of the Deer Tower and shot three arrows from his chariot. He then climbed out and decapitated Zhou Xin's charred body with his yellow axe. The head was impaled upon his great white standard. Next, Wan Wang had Daji, the concubine, brought before him and strangled. Again, he fired three arrows and then decapitated her with his black axe. The adorned head was impaled on his small white standard. Now he was conqueror, but, with all the Imperial Jades ruined by fire, he could not be emperor and father to the people. Then came Weiziqi to Wan Wang's camp, making the traditional gestures of surrender and self-sacrifice. He came naked to the waist, with his hands bound and drawing an empty coffin behind him. In his mouth he held the sacred Sky Ring of Shang. Wan Wang received Weiziqi before his field pavilion. He raised Weiziqi up with his own hands, untied his wrists and accepted from him the ring of blue jade. In an act of mercy, Wan Wang burned the coffin instead of Weiziqi and returned him to his estates in Wei.

Now that Wan Wang was emperor, he restored his empire and reinstituted the ring sacrifices. Peace and prosperity returned to the land. Wan Wang used the Sky Ring of the one true jade of Heaven as it was intended. Heaven and Earth were in harmony once more.

ARABIA AND INDIA

The mythology of the East has innumerable legends dealing with magic rings. In the Arabic world the use of magicians' rings of power was considered even more common than it was in the West. That wonderful anthology of Eastern legends, *One Thousand and One Nights*, contains many tales involving magical rings. The most famous of these is the story of Aladdin's Magical Lamp. In the original story, we find that the genie of Aladdin's ring is far stronger and more useful than the genie of his lamp. The genie gets him into no end of trouble, while the genie of the ring saves his life three times.

In India, the ring is often used as a symbol for the

recognition of divinity in mortals. Among the many ring legends of this kind is one known as "The Bodhisattva's Ring". In this tale, the son of Brahmadatta, the king of Benares, is raised secretly as an untouchable stick-gatherer. The untouchable mother and child are brought to the throne-room. Recognition comes only when his mother throws the child into the air. Bearing a ruby ring in his hand, the child does not fall to the floor, but levitates in the air. The king accepts the child as his true heir and an incarnation of the Buddha.

In India, the quest for the ring can be almost entirely spiritual in nature. This is related to the Indian Vedic tradition, which teaches that the "ring of fire" burns away all ignorance and illusion. The pilgrim or warrior who passes through its flames attains a mystical state of perfect peace. This is like the Buddhist meditational state of Satori. This is the ring of fire at the centre of the universe and the Chidambaram, "the centre of the universe which is within the heart". It is an eternal place without time, where the true state of the soul may be observed and will grow to perfect wisdom.

To some degree, this Vedic ring of fire is comparable to the enchanted ring of fire which Sigurd the Völsung rode through to make his way to his Valkyrie bride. It is also comparable to the Elven rings of enchantment that protected the hidden Elf kingdoms of Lothlórien and Doriath from evil and the march of time. Then there is its evil opposite, the satanic fiery ring that burned round the evil Eye of Sauron and preserved his damned spirit from mortal death.

PART

THIRTEEN

THE ALCHEMIST'S RING

RINGS IN ALCHEMY: A SECRET LANGUAGE

◆

A s touched upon elsewhere in this book, the ring was also the symbol of the alchemist. The alchemist's ring – in the form of a serpent swallowing its own tail – represented a quest for knowledge that was forbidden by the Church. Alchemists were often executed as sorcerers or magicians. The practices of these alchemists were often linked with their rings. The real or imagined use and trade of such "rings of power" were perceived as an evil that must be eradicated.

Because of constant persecution, alchemists cloaked their studies in secrecy and wrote up their experiments and formulae in codified records. The 20th century's leading historian of religions, Mircea Eliade, concluded that alchemical studies were transmitted mystically, just as poetry uses fables and parables. Regarding alchemy, Eliade wrote: "What we are dealing with here is a secret language such as we meet among shamans and secret societies and among the mystics of the traditional religions."

This "secret language" is strongly reminiscent of the *Exeter Book*'s "magic speech" of the ring. It seems likely that we are dealing with the same kind of cryptic communication. The "magic speech" of the ring and the "secret language" of alchemy are one. The dominance of the symbol of the ring in pagan religions – and in all shamanistic tribal cultures who use metal – is related to the ring's alchemical origins.

The symbol for the alchemist was a gold ring in the form of a serpent swallowing its own tail. This serpent ring is the Ouroboros, meaning a "a tail biter", a symbol for eternity that is found in a score of mythologies. In many cultures, we find in the great serpent the first form to emerge from chaos; it then encircles the void and creates time and space by forming a ring, becoming the Ouroboros and grasping its own tail. We see this celestial serpent ring in the Babylonian serpent called Ea, the Greek Ophion, the Hindu Sheshna, the Chinese Naga and the Norse Jörmungandr.

The ring was a symbol of the alchemist's profession and a vision of the alchemist's quest. This was a ring very like that seen in a vision by the 17th-century metaphysical poet Henry Vaughan, in his poem "The World":

> I saw Eternity the other night
> Like a great Ring of pure and endless light,
> All calm, as it was bright,
> And round beneath it, Time in hours, days, years
> Driv'n by the spheres …

To the alchemist, the ring shaped like, or engraved with, the "eternal" serpent and made of "immortal" gold was the symbol for universal knowledge. It was – one might say – the "One Ring" by which all others are ruled.

THE SHAMAN, THE SORCERER AND THE SMITH

The power of the alchemist traditionally evolved through a combination of natural science and supernatural wisdom, which are embodied in the crafts of the shaman and the smith. These are derived from the symbols and mysteries of metallurgy, and are ultimately emblematic of the physical and spiritual mastery of fire.

Traditionally, the alchemist – like the magician and the smith – is given the title "master of fire". The smith's mastery of fire is obvious enough in his forging of metals.

The magician – from the most obscure tribal shaman to
Tolkienian Wizards like Gandalf – handles fire and flame
as a demonstration of mastery of spiritual power. Indeed,
in many cultures the magicians, fakirs and shaman are
traditionally renowned for walking on hot coals and spitting
fire. The alchemist employs both physical and spiritual fire
to transform the natural world.

The Shaman

In Tolkien's world of *The Lord of the Rings*, we have the ultimate evil alchemist in the form of Sauron, the Ring Lord. Sauron is both a magician (or sorcerer) and a smith who forges the supernatural One Ring of Power. He has the perfect evil alchemist's pedigree. He was originally a good fire spirit apprenticed to the Vala Aulë the Smith. He betrayed his master and became the disciple of Melkor, the Dark Sorcerer. Through a combination of his skills as a sorcerer and a smith, he creates the ultimate weapon in his One Ring of Power. We are told that the mortal Easterlings and Southrons saw Sauron as both king and god and feared him, for he surrounded his abode with fire. Sauron built the Dark Tower of Mordor near the fiery volcano of Mount Doom.

THE "ALCHEMICAL" RACES OF MIDDLE-EARTH

There are several other instances of the theme of alchemy in *The Lord of the Rings*.

Many races fall quickly and easily under the spell of the One Ring, but those enemies of Sauron who cannot be immediately enslaved are resilient chiefly because they too possess elements of alchemical power. These are the Noldor Elves, the Dwarves and the Númenóreans.

The greatest of these are the Noldor Elves, who are already gifted with "Elven magic" before they become the students and disciples of Aulë the Smith. (In Tolkien's original drafts the Noldor were actually called the Gnomes, from the Greek *genomos*, meaning "earth-dweller"; while Noldor is Elvish for "knowledge", just as Gnostic – the alchemical sect – is from the Greek *gnosis*, meaning "knowledge".) Greatest of the Noldor Elves is Fëanor (meaning "spirit of fire"), who

in *The Silmarillion* combines Elvish spells and smith's skills to forge the famous Silmarils. These are the "jewels of light" stolen by Sauron's master, Melkor, the Lord of Darkness, and over which the wars of the First Age are fought. Fëanor's grandson is the Noldor prince Celebrimbor, the Lord of the Elven-smiths of Eregion, who forges the Rings of Power, over which the wars of the Second and Third Ages are fought.

The Dwarves are also tough opponents who possess elements of alchemical power, for they are a race who were shaped by Aulë the Smith. They are resilient to fire both physical and sorcerous. They are a stubborn race who mark their weapons and armour with Dwarf runes and spells. The greatest of the Dwarves was Telchar the

Smith, whose weapons are blessed with such powers that one (the knife called Angrist) is used to cut a Silmaril from Melkor's (Morgoth's) iron crown; and another (the sword Narsil) is used to cut the One Ring from Sauron's hand.

The Númenóreans and their Dúnedain descendants on Middle-earth learn their alchemical skills from the Noldar Elves and the Dwarves, and in some creations even outdo their masters. So, as the Dúnedain of the North and the Men of Gondor are the surviving descendants of these great people, and the chief inheritors of ancient wisdom which gives them the power to resist evil temptation, these people are seen by Sauron as the chief obstacles to his dominion of Middle-earth. However, there are also the Istari, or Wizards, who have been sent by the Valar to Middle-earth as adversaries of Sauron the Ring Lord. Yet, of the five Wizards who came, only Gandalf is able to stand against Sauron. For it is Gandalf wearing Narya – the Elf "ring of fire" – who best understands the alchemical nature of the conflict with Sauron. It is Gandalf who discovers and translates the "secret language" of the One Ring which is "written in fire".

GOOD AND BAD ALCHEMY

◆

Gandalf's Elf Ring and Sauron's One Ring are both symbolic of the control of alchemical fire, but alchemical fire of different types. The evil alchemy that made the One Ring commands the dark satanic fire out of the bowels of the earth. This power transforms the material world – or at least gives that illusion – and the accompanying illusion of world power. The good alchemy of Gandalf's Elf ring commands the celestial fire of the spirit. This "good" alchemical fire has no

Opposite: The Fathers of Dwarves fashioned by Aulë the Smith

power over the material world. However, the fire of the spirit does have the power to impassion and uplift the soul because ultimately its source is the sacred "Flame Imperishable" of Eru the One – the Supreme Being who gave all things life.

This head-on conflict, of course, leads to mutual destruction. Gandalf foresees this, but makes the sacrifice because no other way is possible. However, Gandalf also understands that, ultimately, the only way to defeat Sauron and his evil One Ring is not to attempt to overthrow him or to seize its power, but to undo the alchemical process by which the Ring of Power has been made. Once Gandalf understands the "language of the ring", he knows that only by reversing the alchemical process can Sauron be defeated. Just as common folklore tells us one can undo a spell by reciting it backward, so Gandalf understood that the only way the One Ring could be destroyed was to reverse the process by which it was made. This was the reason for *The Lord of the Rings'* "backward" ring quest. The One Ring had to be taken back to the crucible where it was made. Only there in the fiery furnace of the "Cracks of Doom" where it was forged could the One Ring be unmade – and Sauron's power destroyed.

In its creation, Sauron's One Ring was the ultimate heresy against the alchemical tradition. It was the evil opposite of the Ouroboros, or serpent ring of the alchemist. When Sauron came to the Elven-smiths of Middle-earth and persuaded them to forge the other Rings of Power, he came in disguise as Annatar, "giver of gifts". He appeared as a benevolent alchemist very like the Greek hero Prometheus. But he was, in fact, the exact opposite. Prometheus's ring marked the saviour who enslaved himself and gave mortals freedom, knowledge and life. Sauron's ring marked the tyrant who enslaved the world and gave mortals bondage, ignorance and death.

Opposite: The One Ring forged in the fires of Mount Doom by Sauron the Dark Lord

THE CONTRIBUTION OF GNOSTICISM

When considering the alchemist tradition of the serpent ring, the Ouroboros, it is essential to recognize that it was also the symbol of the early Christian religion and philosophy known as Gnosticism. In the Fourth Book of the Gnostic text *Pistis Sophia*, Jesus tells the Virgin Mary: "The Outer darkness is a great serpent, the tail of which is in its mouth, and it is outside the whole world, and surroundeth the whole world."

Gnosticism also taught that the serpent and the Christ were interchangeable figures, and that both were saviours or "redeemers".

By the 1st century CE, Gnostic religion and Western alchemical doctrine were largely indistinguishable. This eventually proved to be unfortunate for the older tradition of alchemy. Gnosticism became such a successful competitor for converts that St John and St Paul constantly railed against (and shamelessly libelled) its missionaries and saints. Later Christians so ruthlessly suppressed Gnostic teachings that the possession of an Ouroboros ring was sufficient grounds for the charge of heresy and sorcery. The result was that even after the virtual extermination of Gnosticism by the 6th century, Christian fanatics tended to view the alchemist's ring as a satanic relic.

Naturally enough, in the hostile world of Christian suppression, the already obscure and symbolic language of the alchemist and Gnostic became even more veiled and secretive.

APOLLONIUS OF TYANA — TALKING TO RINGS

Going back to the "language of the ring", it is interesting to look at this idea historically in relation to the many beliefs in the power of rings that have permeated our culture. An important example was one of the major historical figures in alchemy and Gnosticism, Apollonius of Tyana. Apollonius was a learned man who in the 1st century CE had been initiated into the famous Pythagorean cult mysteries of Greece, along with some of the wisest men of his age. After many years of study, he then observed five years of silence and wandered into the lands of the Indian Brahmans, where he gained even greater knowledge and wisdom. There he is said to have received seven rings as a gift from the Brahman master and Indian prince Iarchus. Each ring was marked with a different stone, and Apollonius wore them one by one in order of the days of the week, "for it is said that he revered them as divine, so that he changed them each day and made them partakers of his greatest secrets."

Historical evidence suggests Apollonius was a blamelessly compassionate scholar who brought healing and knowledge to many during his lifetime. Yet he became the victim of 15

Opposite: Three Elven Rings: Vilya the Blue Ring of Air, Narya the Red Ring of Fire and Nenya the White Ring of Water

centuries of Christian attack. So vilified was he in Christian propaganda that his ring consultations began to sound rather like Tolkien's evil character Gollum, who insanely talked to his "precious" evil ring. Tolkien tells us that the One Ring seemed to possess Gollum more than Gollum possessed the Ring, and that "he talked to it, even when it was not with him".

What is behind all this business of "talking to rings"? Are these testimonies about people communing with spirits in rings total fabrications made up to condemn Christian heretics? Or was there some real basis for these strange accusations?

Looking more closely at the case of Apollonius, it is very likely that Apollonius of Tyana did "consult" his rings, as was rumoured. Furthermore, in a very real sense, those seven rings did in fact contain much of his secret knowledge. And as he was a renowned teacher, we are told – probably correctly – that when others came under his influence, they also acquired similar "magic rings" which they too would consult in the manner of their master.

THE ART OF MEMORY

As the historical scholar Frances Yates recorded in her book *The Art of Memory*, the primary and often sole means of teaching in ancient and medieval times was oral, and knowledge was retained by human memory alone. For even with the advent of literate scholars and handwritten books and records, it was not until the invention of the printing press that knowledge had any broad circulation outside of oral teaching traditions. For the majority of Europe's population up to the 19th century, it remained the primary means of learning.

Consequently, the first priority of all scholars or potential scholars was the acquisition of a system of memory by which knowledge acquired could be stored and retrieved when needed. Every teaching institution or sect had a system of some kind. These systems varied widely in shape and complexity. Most often, Frances Yates suggests, they took on an architectural form, such as massive temples with extensive grounds and gardens. Each part of the building represented a different category within which information about a different art or science would be stored. Within these larger systems were often smaller ones involving staircases, ladders, ropes and even rings.

It is quite obvious that Apollonius taught an alchemist memory system that was a kind of "ring oracle" or an intellectual's form of dactylomancy. It was a memory system where each ring was a catalogue file to a library of Gnostic and alchemical knowledge.

So, strangely enough, these recurring accusations of sorcery by consulting rings begin to make some sense.

The problem was that the early Christian opponents of Gnosticism were primarily fundamentalist and anti-intellectual in nature. Christian archbishops proudly burned ancient Greco-Roman libraries, closed universities and drove scholars into exile. Many scholars had to flee to Baghdad and other parts of the Muslim world. Indeed, if it had not been for the tolerance and intellectual enlightenment of the leaders of Islam at this time, much of the art, science and literature of the ancient Greco-Roman civilization would have been lost forever. The madness and paranoia of fundamentalist Christianity emerged again and again throughout the Middle Ages and inevitably resulted in the persecution of anyone with intellectual pretensions who was not directly under the protection of the Church.

Consequently, it is easy to see how charges about alchemists and other scholars "speaking with devils" imprisoned in rings could gain currency. However, from such a simplistic point of view, any kind of memory system or recitation used to retain and pass on knowledge was suspect.

CELEBRIMBOR AND THE FORGING OF THE RINGS OF POWER

Mahtan — "Copper Lover"

Míriel — "Jewel Daughter"

Finwë, *High King of the Noldor*

Nerdanel the Wise — *Sculptor*

Fëanor — "Spirit of Fire," maker of the Silmarils

Curufin — "Skillful Son"

Celebrimbor — "Silver Fist," *forger of the Rings of Power*

NINE RINGS OF MEN (CELEBRIMBOR)

SEVEN RINGS OF DWARVES (CELEBRIMBOR)

THREE RINGS OF ELVES (CELEBRIMBOR)

The Witch-king of Angmar *(a Black Númenórean)*

The lesser Black Númenóreans

Khamûl *the Black Easterling*

The Easterlings and Southrons

Vilya the blue Ring of Air

Narya the red Ring of Fire

Nenya the white Ring of Water

Elrond

Galadriel

Cirdan

Longbeards *(Durin's Folk)*

Broadbeams

Firebeards

Ironfists

Stiffbeards

Blacklocks

Stonefoots

THE ONE RING (SAURON)

PART

FOURTEEN

WAGNER'S
RING

Richard Wagner's first performance of *The Ring of the Nibelung* in 1876 has often been cited as the first great expression of the identity of the recently unified German nation. Certainly, Wagner saw art as a political as well as an aesthetic act, and with his epic music drama he was attempting to claim a mythological heritage and a national art. For Wagner, art and myth were linked. He believed that true art must arise from the primordial depths of a people's collective being, the *Volk*. *The Ring of the Nibelung* was a purposeful act of making a statement of German identity and claiming the root of that identity was to be found in the Germanic epic tradition of the ring quest myths.

Criticized as Wagner may be for his manipulations and distortions of Norse myth and medieval German literature, it was his genius which recognized the significance of the ring myth, and the importance of reclaiming it for his own time. Furthermore, one must recognize that Wagner's opera brilliantly conveys the huge spirit of this ancient tale on a truly epic scale. Just as the *Völsunga Saga* and *The Nibelungenlied* were interpretations of the quest appropriate to their times, so Wagner's *The Ring of the Nibelung* was true to the spirit of his time.

THE RHINEGOLD

SCENE ONE

In the limpid green depths of a river, the three water nymphs – the Rhinemaidens – play and sing. These are the beautiful daughters of the River Rhine, who are spied on by Alberich the Nibelung. The ugly dwarf has made his way down into their watery realm, where he lustfully and fruitlessly pursues the teasing nymphs. Enraged by their mocking, the dwarf is suddenly overcome by a brilliant golden glow. Rays of sunlight catch on a gold pinnacle of rock, which fills the murky river with shimmering gold light. The nymphs sing praises to this treasure, the Rhinegold, which is a stone that, if forged into a gold ring, would allow its master to become lord of the world.

However, the Rhinegold can be taken and mastered only by one who is willing to curse love and renounce all love's pleasures. Since Alberich is too ugly to win love anyway, he will take power: he swears an oath renouncing love. The Nibelung then snatches the Rhinegold from the pinnacle and flees into the dark.

SCENE TWO

Dawn comes to a mountain height above the Rhine Valley where Wotan, the king of the gods, and his queen, Fricka, sleep. In the distance stands a magnificent castle with gleaming battlements, up on an impossibly high peak. Fricka wakes Wotan, and the god is filled with delight at the sight of the newly completed kingdom of the gods. This was a realm built by the brute force of giants, but conceived in Wotan's dreams.

Unfortunately, the price promised to the giants Fasolt and Fafner for building this kingdom is the hand of Fricka's sister, Freia, the goddess of youth. However, with Freia the gods will also lose the golden apples of immortality of which she is guardian, and, without this fruit, they will soon grow old and die.

When the giants come for their payment, Donner, the god of thunder, Froh, the god of spring, and Loge, the trickster god of fire, come to side with Wotan to defend Freia. But the bargain cannot be broken as Wotan has sworn to make payment upon his sacred spear of law. It is up to Loge to come up with an alternative payment. The giants agree: they will have the ring of the Nibelung which Alberich has forged from the stolen Rhinegold, along with all the golden treasures he has amassed through its power. Loge also reveals that, if the ring is not soon taken from Alberich, he will rule over all of them anyway. The giants take Freia as a hostage, as Wotan and Loge descend into the bowels of the earth in search of the realm of Alberich the Nibelung.

SCENE THREE

The subterranean caverns of Nibelheim, the home of the Nibelung dwarfs, are a vast stone labyrinth of tunnels and chambers. This is a dark and sinister world lit only by the red glow of furnace and forge. Here, Alberich the ring lord torments his enslaved brother Mime, who has just completed the forging of the magic helmet called Tarnhelm on Alberich's orders. Tarnhelm has the power to make the wearer invisible or change him into whatever form he wishes. It can also transport him to any place he wishes. Alberich places the Tarnhelm on his head and immediately vanishes. The invisible Alberich then cruelly kicks and beats Mime until he cries out for mercy. Delighted with his new toy, Alberich goes off to terrorize his other enslaved dwarfs.

Mime continues to bewail his enslavement, as the gods Wotan and Loge enter the cavern. Alberich soon returns, driving his treasure-bearing dwarfs before him. They pile up a huge hoard of purest gold. Alberich contemptuously greets his guests and arrogantly reveals how he will build up such vast wealth and power that he will eventually overthrow the gods and rule the world.

Wotan can barely contain his anger, but crafty Loge flatters the dwarf and asks him about the powers of Tarnhelm. "Can it really transform him into any shape?" he asks. "Certainly," Alberich replies, and immediately becomes a huge dragon. Loge feigns fear and astonishment, but then suggests that it would surely be more impressive if the dwarf could become something really small, like a toad. Alberich foolishly obliges and transforms himself into a tiny toad. Wotan immediately seizes the tiny toad, while Loge snatches up Tarnhelm. When Alberich resumes his usual shape, he is bound and dragged off as a captive.

SCENE FOUR

The bound Alberich is taken to the misty mountain height above the Rhine where the bargain with the giants was struck. In order to win his freedom, Alberich is forced to give up his hoard of gold, Tarnhelm, and his magic ring. The enraged dwarf refuses, but finally everything is taken from him. Once the humiliated Alberich is released, he wrathfully places a curse of disaster and death on anyone who commands the ring. Soon after, all the gods gather with the giants, Fasolt and Fafner, and their hostage Freia. Fasolt is in love with Freia, but agrees to accept gold only if it completely hides her from his sight. The gods pile all the gold around her, but Fasolt can still see the sheen of her hair, so Loge gives up Tarnhelm to cover it. She seems entirely covered, but Fasolt cries out that he can still see the star-like glint of her eye. The giants demand the ring to seal the crack, but Wotan is enthralled by the ring's power and will not give it up. Loge meanwhile tries to claim it for its rightful owners, the Rhinemaidens.

In the midst of the quarrel, the earth splits open and Erda, goddess of the earth, arises out of the ground. She is the spirit of the world and the prophet of the gods. She commands Wotan to surrender the ring or the gods and all their realm will be doomed. Almost immediately the curse of the ring strikes when the giants quarrel over its possession. Fafner brutally murders Fasolt and takes both the ring and the treasure. After Fafner's departure, Donner, god of thunder, walks into the mountain mists, where the thunder of his hammer is heard and flashes of lightning are seen as he forges a rainbow bridge. It arches through the air and leads up to the great castle of the gods, which Wotan now names Valhalla. Wotan leads the godly procession over the Rainbow Bridge to Valhalla, while far below the Rhinemaidens cry out for the loss of their gold.

THE VALKYRIE

ACT ONE
SCENE ONE

A storm is raging, and the hero Siegmund the Walsung enters the great hall of the warrior-chieftain Hunding. In the middle of the dwelling is the trunk of a huge ash tree whose limbs support the roof. He is wounded and exhausted from pursuit by enemies through the forest. He collapses on a bearskin before the fire in the enormous stone hearth. Hunding's wife, Sieglinde, enters the house and, seeing the now unconscious Siegmund, takes pity on him and revives him. Instantly, there is a powerful attraction between the two.

SCENE TWO

Hunding arrives home and reluctantly offers shelter and food to Siegmund. When he asks Siegmund his name, the youth gives his outlaw name, Wehwalt the Wolfing. His name means "Woeful": his father, Wolfe, his mother and his twin sister were all slain or lost to him. As he describes his latest disasters, it is soon revealed that his enemies are Hunding's kinsmen. Hunding tells his guest he is safe for the night, but in the morning he must find a weapon and they will duel to the death.

SCENE THREE

Alone in the great hall, Siegmund is soon joined by Sieglinde, who has given Hunding a sleeping-potion. Sieglinde tells Siegmund how she had been orphaned as a child, and as a captive was given as a reluctant bride to Hunding. But to the wedding came a stranger: an old man dressed all in grey with a slouch hat and a single glittering eye. That old man brought a bright sword and drove it into the mighty ash tree that holds up the roof of Hunding's house. Many heroes since that time have tried to draw it out, but none could do it. When Sieglinde confesses her unhappiness, Siegmund swears his love for her and promises to free her from her forced marriage. As Sieglinde swears her love in return, they tell one another more about their past lives. When the hero reveals that his father's real name was Walse, Sieglinde suddenly realizes that he is her long-lost twin brother, and their passion for one another is redoubled. Siegmund draws the gleaming sword from the great ash tree as the two lovers rejoice in this union of Walsung blood. They then rush out into the night.

ACT TWO
SCENE ONE

In a craggy mountainous wilderness, the mighty Wotan talks to his Valkyrie daughter Brunnhilde and tells her she must go into battle and give a just victory to his mortal son, Siegmund the Walsung, over Hunding. Joyfully, she obeys him and departs, just as Wotan's queen Fricka arrives upon a chariot drawn by two rams in the wake of a storm. Queen Fricka, who is also the goddess of marriage, insists that Hunding's sacred marriage rights must be defended and the Walsungs punished for adultery and incest. Wotan is forced against his will to enforce the law, for his power will leave him if he does not. Wotan swears an oath to command the death of Siegmund the Walsung. Queen Fricka victoriously rides off in her chariot.

SCENE TWO

Angered and saddened, Wotan now tells the Valkyrie Brunnhilde how Valhalla was bought with the ring, and how the ring was doubly cursed by dwarfs and Rhinemaidens. To prevent disaster, Wotan went to the goddess Erda, with whom he conceived the nine Valkyries, who would gather in Valhalla a vast army of heroes to help defend the gods in their hour of need. Yet the fate of the world is dependent on Alberich's ring, for the dwarf of Nibelheim still plots continually to seize the ring from the giant Fafner, who broods over his golden treasure and guards it night and day. If the Nibelung eventually seizes the ring, the fate of the gods will be sealed. For by its power, Alberich will turn Wotan's heroic army against him and overthrow the gods. As Wotan is forbidden the ring, and only Alberich who has cursed love can command its power, the only hope

for the gods is to be found in a mortal hero who is brave and strong enough to slay the giant and seize the ring on their behalf. To this end, the mortal hero Siegmund the Walsung was conceived and given a godly sword called Notung. But the curse of the ring is at work, for the laws of Fricka dictate that Wotan must order Brunnhilde to slay Siegmund.

SCENE THREE

The Valkyrie Brunnhilde sees Siegmund and Sieglinde approaching a rocky gorge and slips away. Siegmund comforts his sister-bride, who hears the hunting-horn of Hunding in pursuit and tells Siegmund to leave her and flee. Siegmund will not and swears to protect her with his sword, Notung, and tenderly comforts her until she falls into an exhausted sleep.

SCENE FOUR

Brunnhilde appears as if in a vision to Siegmund, leading her horse. Only warriors condemned to die can see the Valkyries, and Brunnhilde tells Siegmund that she will take him to Valhalla. Siegmund says he will not leave his sister-bride for the warriors' heaven. The Valkyrie tells him he has no choice, but Siegmund says he will make sure they are together in death. He takes out his sword with the intention of slaying both Sieglinde and himself. The Valkyrie stays his hand and swears she will violate the will of Wotan and give victory to Siegmund the Walsung.

SCENE FIVE

Siegmund leaves the sleeping Sieglinde and goes in search of Hunding. As the storm clouds flash and roar, the battle between the heroes commences upon a distant mountain

Opposite: Fafner the Dragon

ridge. Sieglinde wakes and is tormented by the sight of the conflict. Siegmund is protected by the Valkyrie's shield, and Hunding is driven back. But just as Brunnhilde guides Siegmund's sword in what would certainly be a fatal blow, the storm clouds part and throb with fiery light. The fierce Wotan appears; he stands over Hunding and blocks Siegmund's stroke with the shaft of his spear. Siegmund's sword shatters and Hunding immediately plunges his own spear into the unarmed Siegmund's breast. Brunnhilde, seeing the hero lost, swiftly lifts Sieglinde onto her steed and rides away. Wotan remains sadly looking over the body of his mortal son Siegmund. Hunding pulls his spear from Siegmund's body, but stands too near the god. With a contemptuous wave of his hand, Wotan strikes Hunding dead then vanishes in a flash of lightning.

ACT THREE
SCENE ONE

On the craggy heights of the Valkyrie Rock, the Valkyries arrive one by one with dead warriors across their saddles. The eight shield maidens gather to await Brunnhilde before they ride off to Valhalla. They are astonished when they see the rebel Valkyrie arrive with a living maiden across her saddle. They are filled with fear when they are told what has occurred. Sieglinde despairs and does not wish to live until Brunnhilde tells her that she is carrying Siegmund's child. For this she is thankful and determined to live. She takes the shards of the hero's sword from the Valkyrie, who also tells her that her son's name is to be Siegfried – victorious and free. Sieglinde is told to escape into the pine forest below the rock because Wotan avoids this place. In it lives the evil giant Fafner, who, after long years of brooding over his treasure and his ring, has become a great dragon. Sieglinde flees, while Brunnhilde bravely awaits Wotan's wrath.

SCENE TWO

Wotan appears before the Valkyries in a flash of fiery red light. In his fury he condemns Brunnhilde: she will lose all her supernatural powers and become a mortal man's wife. The other Valkyries are filled with horror at their sister's fate and beg Wotan to have pity on her. Wotan silences them and drives them away by threatening them with the same fate.

SCENE THREE

Wotan and Brunnhilde remain alone on the rock. She claims that in defying his command she was actually doing his will and protecting his favourite mortal children, the Walsungs. But Wotan cannot take back his judgment. He tells her that he will cast a spell of sleep on her. She will be left upon this rock for any mortal man to find, and when she is awakened she will be his prize. Wotan sadly and tenderly kisses Brunnhilde's eyes, and she falls into an enchanted sleep. Wotan lays her gently upon the ground, closes the visor of her helmet over her face and places her Valkyrie shield over her breast. Invoking Loge's fire, Wotan encircles the rock where the sleeping beauty lies with a wall of flame. Striking the rock as he departs, Wotan invokes a spell forbidding the rock to anyone who fears his spear.

SIEGFRIED

ACT ONE
SCENE ONE

A large cave on the edge of a deep wood serves as a smithy for that ill-humoured dwarf Mime, the brother of Alberich. Mime toils at the forge, complaining about his ungrateful foster son, Siegfried. The greedy dwarf has no love for the powerful youth, but his plan is to get Siegfried to slay the dragon Fafner who lives nearby and so win the ring and treasure for Mime. The problem is that Mime doesn't have the skill to re-forge the sword Notung, and all the swords he makes are not strong enough for the youth. Dressed in skins, the young Siegfried enters the smithy leading a huge bear on a rope, and jokingly has the bear chase the smith about the cave until he gives him his new sword. Once again, when Siegfried tries the blade, it breaks, and the youth scolds the dwarf. Siegfried wonders at his dislike of this dwarf who has nurtured him; something has always told him that Mime is evil. After threats from Siegfried, Mime finally tells the youth how his mother, Sieglinde, died in childbirth. Siegfried demands proof, so Mime shows him the fragments of the sword Notung. Siegfried rejoices and orders Mime to re-forge the sword.

SCENE TWO

An ancient one-eyed man in a dark blue cloak enters the smithy. He is weary from his travels and uses a spear as a staff and wears a large broad-brimmed hat. He is called the Wanderer but is actually Wotan in his earthly guise, and he asks the inhospitable Mime for shelter. The dwarf

Opposite: Wotan the Wanderer

tries to turn the traveller from his door, but the Wanderer challenges him to a contest of riddles, which will result in the loser giving up his head. The Wanderer easily answers Mime's three riddles – who lives under the earth (the dwarfs or black-elves of Nibelheim), on it (the giants of Riesenheim) and above it (the gods or light spirits of Valhalla)? In return, Mime answers two of the Wanderer's riddles – name the family that Wotan loved best yet treated most harshly (the Wasungs), and name the sword of the Walsungs (Notung). However, when the Wanderer asks him to name the one who can re-forge Notung, Mime is beaten. The answer to the riddle is: only one who has never known fear can re-forge the sword. To that same man, the Wanderer says, as he departs, he will leave the forfeit of Mime's head.

SCENE THREE

Siegfried returns for his sword and finds it not yet made. Mime now understands that Siegfried is the "one who has never known fear" and desperately tries to teach him the "meaning of fear". This proves impossible, so Mime suggests that they go to visit Fafner the dragon, so the youth might learn about fear. Siegfried is keen to learn this new sensation, but decides that he must re-forge his father's sword himself as Mime cannot. With sheer barbaric energy and demon strength, Siegfried succeeds where Mime has failed. As he works at the forge, the dwarf cooks up a sleeping potion for the youth. He believes that the youth will now slay Fafner the dragon, so the only way Mime may win the ring and save his life is to drug the youth and slay him while he sleeps. At last, the frenzy at the forge comes to a halt. Siegfried holds up the brilliant re-forged blade of Notung. Then, with a single stroke, he splits the anvil in two.

ACT TWO
SCENE ONE

In the depths of a forest in the dark of night, Alberich the Nibelung watches Fafner's cave and broods over the ring. Wotan the Wanderer greets him in the dark. Alberich immediately recognizes him, but the god assures the dwarf that he is not after the ring. He warns Alberich that his real rival is his brother Mime. The young Siegfried knows nothing of the dragon's gold and the ring, and Wotan is banned from informing or helping him. Then the Wanderer calls out to wake the dragon. Both the Wanderer and Alberich offer to save Fafner's life in exchange for the ring, but the dragon finds this a ridiculous offer. He fears no one and goes back to sleep. Wotan laughs as he departs, telling Alberich he woke the dragon only to show the dwarf how fate cannot be altered.

SCENE TWO

As day breaks, Siegfried and Mime climb to a knoll above the mouth of the dragon's cave. Mime leaves Siegfried alone and the youth blows his horn and wakes the dragon. Surprised, but not alarmed by Fafner's size, Siegfried jokes with the monster and then asks him if he might teach him fear. The dragon grows impatient with the cocky youth and a titanic struggle ensues. The battle ends when Siegfried pierces the monster's heart. As Fafner dies, he warns the youth of the ring's curse. He also tells the hero that, because of the ring, Siegfried will also soon die. Some of the dragon's blood drips on Siegfried's fingers and he puts

Next page: The mountain road to Valkyrie Rock

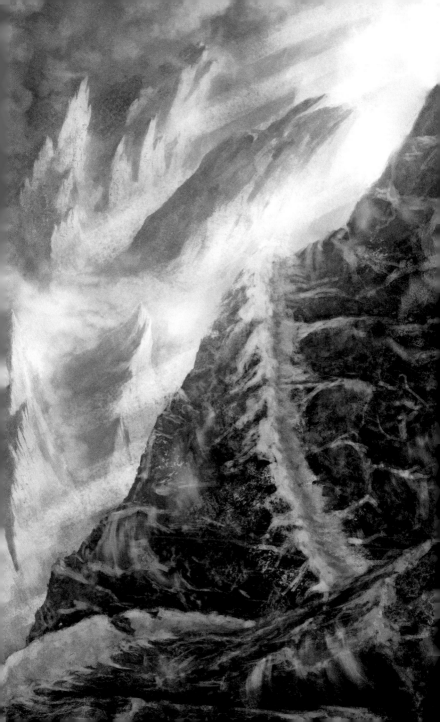

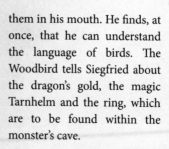

them in his mouth. He finds, at once, that he can understand the language of birds. The Woodbird tells Siegfried about the dragon's gold, the magic Tarnhelm and the ring, which are to be found within the monster's cave.

SCENE THREE

The dwarf brothers Alberich and Mime emerge from hiding. Seeing Fafner dead, they begin at once to argue over who will claim the treasure. Siegfried emerges from the dragon's cave with the ring on his hand and Tarnhelm tied to his belt. The Woodbird now warns him about Mime's plot. When Mime approaches and offers Siegfried a poisoned drink, the young hero cuts the dwarf's head off, as Alberich laughs in the distance. Siegfried blocks the treasure-cave door with the body of the dragon. He then sets out on a new adventure when he is told by the Woodbird about a sleeping maiden who is to be found surrounded by a ring of fire on Valkyrie Rock.

ACT THREE
SCENE ONE

In a wild mountain pass, Wotan in his earthly guise as the Wanderer summons the prophetic goddess Erda and demands to learn the fate of the gods. When Erda will not give an answer, Wotan accepts that the doom of Valhalla is near. His remaining hope lies with the young hero Siegfried – who now holds the ring – and with Brunnhilde. He bequeaths the world to the Walsungs, and the race of mortal men.

SCENE TWO

In the midst of the god's reverie, Siegfried approaches. The Wanderer detains him and blocks his path. With a single stroke of the re-forged Notung, Siegfried shatters Wotan's spear shaft. Thunder and lightning flash at his deed, and the Wanderer vanishes. Siegfried goes on his way and is soon confronted by the wall of fire. He blows his horn and plunges fearlessly into the flames.

SCENE THREE

Siegfried emerges from the flames at Valkyrie Rock, where he finds the sleeping, armoured warrior. However, when he removes the armour, he discovers the maiden Brunnhilde and is overwhelmed by her beauty. For the first time, he claims to understand what fear is, but he controls his trembling and wakens the sleeping beauty with a kiss. Brunnhilde awakens to her lover. She soon realizes that, by surrendering to Siegfried, she will lose her immortality, but she does so joyfully.

THE TWILIGHT OF THE GODS

PROLOGUE

Flames light up the Valkyrie Rock where the three fatal sisters, the Norns, sing of the ancient days of Wotan's great deeds, as they weave the golden cord of fate. They sing of the shattering of Wotan's spear of law and how this released Loge the god of fire, whose flames will soon consume Valhalla. They attempt to learn when the end will come, but the cord snaps. They understand that their own end has come, and they flee in terror to the caverns of Erda. As dawn comes, Siegfried and his bride Brunnhilde emerge from their cave. Although she is afraid that she may lose her lover, Brunnhilde knows how a warrior's heart yearns for adventure. She gives him her armour and her horse Grane to help in his quest. Siegfried swears his eternal love and gives Brunnhilde the ring as his constant pledge before he sets off into the Rhine valley.

ACT ONE
SCENE ONE

Gunther, the king of the Gibichungs, and his sister Gutrune sit enthroned in the vast hall of their castle on the Rhine. They are in council with their dark, brooding half-brother Hagen, who advises them how they may increase the Gibichung dynasty's wealth and power. He tells them they both must soon marry: Gunther to the wise and beautiful Brunnhilde, and Gutrune to Siegfried the Dragonslayer, who possesses the treasure of the Nibelung gold. This can be achieved only by guile. They agree that, when the approaching hero comes, Gutrune will give him a magic potion that will make Siegfried forget Brunnhilde and fall in love with Gutrune.

SCENE TWO

Siegfried's horn sounds from a river boat as he approaches the castle. Hagen and Gunther welcome him with friendship and honour, and Gutrune brings to him a horned cup filled with the magic potion. Though he toasts them in the name of his lover Brunnhilde, the moment after the drink leaves his lips he opens his eyes and heart to Gutrune. He swears his undying love for her and asks for her hand in marriage. Gunther agrees on the condition that Siegfried win for him the fair Brunnhilde, whose name now means nothing to the drugged Siegfried. Hagen advises Siegfried that they may achieve their aim with the Tarnhelm, by whose magic he may change his shape to that of Gunther. Gunther and Siegfried swear blood oaths of brotherhood and ride off on their adventure.

SCENE THREE

On the Valkyrie Rock, Brunnhilde calls out a greeting of welcome to a sister Valkyrie. But the Valkyrie brings news of disorder and degeneration in Valhalla since Wotan's spear was shattered. Wotan has no authority to rule or act, and nothing will lift the curse of the ring except its return to its rightful guardians. But Brunnhilde angrily refuses to return the ring to the Rhinemaidens, and drives her sister away. The ring is the token of Siegfried's love and nothing will make her part with it. After the Valkyrie's departure, however, a strange man penetrates the flames of the wall of fire. It is Siegfried wearing Tarnhelm, which has changed him to Gunther's form. As Gunther the Gibichung, he claims Brunnhilde as his bride because he has passed the test of the ring of fire. After he seizes the ring from her hand, Brunnhilde has no power to resist him. He carries her off into the cave as his bride, but resolves to lay his sword between them as they sleep, so as not to dishonour his blood-brother.

ACT TWO
SCENE ONE

In front of the Gibichung hall, on the bank of the Rhine, Hagen, armed with spear and shield, is leaning against a doorpost, asleep. It is dark, but in the moonlight Alberich the Nibelung appears to Hagen in a dream. It is revealed that Hagen is the son of Alberich from a loveless union with Gunther's mother. Alberich makes his unhappy son swear that he will win back the Nibelung's ring.

SCENE TWO

As dawn breaks, Hagen awakens and Siegfried joyfully returns and greets him and Gutrune with the news that he has won Brunnhilde for King Gunther. He tells how he remained faithful that night, and then how on the journey back Gunther came and took Siegfried's place, while Siegfried used the power of Tarnhelm to reach the Gibichung castle ahead of them.

SCENE THREE

Hagen has summoned all the vassals of the kingdom to welcome King Gunther and his new queen. They offer up sacrifices to the altars of the gods and swear to uphold the new queen's honour.

SCENE FOUR

When Gunther arrives to present his new bride, Brunnhilde sees Siegfried with the ring upon his hand. She realizes at once that Gunther treacherously won her by deception. She tells all that Siegfried the Walsung is her true husband. Siegfried swears upon the point of Hagen's spear that he has never known this woman as a bride. Brunnhilde is inflamed with a sense of betrayal and swears that his oath is false and that his sword hung on the wall, not between them. Siegfried denies the charge and leaves with Gutrune, although the vassals clearly believe Brunnhilde's story.

SCENE FIVE

Brunnhilde is devastated and bent on vengeance for her betrayal. She turns to Hagen, and tells him that Siegfried is protected from all weapons by a magic spell she wove. There is one way Siegfried may be slain, however; because she knew he would never flee from battle, the spell does not protect his back. So if Hagen drives his spear blade into Siegfried's back, he will die. Brunnhilde's taunts, and Hagen's promises of wealth and power, eventually persuade Gunther to join in the conspiracy to murder, as Siegfried's wedding procession passes by.

ACT THREE
SCENE ONE

In a woodland on the banks of the Rhine, the three Rhinemaidens lament their lost gold. When Siegfried, who is out hunting, appears, they plead that he give back the ring, but he refuses. They warn him that, if he does not return it to the Rhine, he will be slain this day.

SCENE TWO

When the rest of the hunting party arrives, Hagen and Gunther urge Siegfried to entertain them with tales of his childhood with Mime and his slaying of Fafner the Dragon. Finally, after giving him a drink to revive his memory, Hagen asks him to tell of the wooing of Brunnhilde. With a pretence of moral outrage, Hagen drives his spear into the hero's back. Calling out his love for Brunnhilde with his last breath, Siegfried dies.

SCENE THREE

In front of the Gibichung hall in the moonlight, Gutrune is anxiously waiting as an evil dream wakes her in the night. Hagen comes to tell her that Siegfried has been killed by a wild boar. However, when his body is carried in, Gutrune will have none of it. She accuses Gunther of murder, but Gunther denies it and curses Hagen. Hagen defiantly admits the murder, but says it was justice. Then he claims the golden ring for himself. When Gunther disputes his right, Hagen slays him. Yet when he is about to seize the ring, the dead Siegfried's hand rises threateningly against him. Hagen falls back in fear, as Brunnhilde commands all to stand back from the hero. She orders a funeral pyre to be made for Siegfried. She then takes the ring and places it on her own finger. Then Brunnhilde torches the pyre, calls on the Rhinemaidens to retrieve the gold from the ashes, then rides Grane into the flames. The Rhine overflows its banks as the Gibichung hall is also consumed in the flames. The Rhinemaidens rise with the river. They joyfully seize the ring, and vengefully drag the damned Hagen down to a watery grave. The flood subsides to leave only the burned ruin of the hall, but in the distance, in the heavens, Valhalla can be seen catching alight, and is finally entirely consumed by flames.

PART

FIFTEEN

TOLKIEN IN
THE 20TH
CENTURY

n *The Ring Legends of Tolkien*, the symbol of the ring and the tradition of the ring quest has been looked at through the millennia. It is clear how Tolkien drew on the myth, history and literature of a score of cultures in the creation of his multilayered epic *The Lord of the Rings*.

Without rejecting its heritage, however, Tolkien radically transformed the ring quest and made it into something fresh and relevant to the 20th century.

Each age has its use for the ring quest, and special circumstances or "accidents of history" in the 20th century have made Tolkien's version of that quest not only relevant and meaningful but, to some degree, prophetic. That is not to say that *The Lord of the Rings* is an allegory of our time. Tolkien rightly rejected the allegorical view as too narrow for his tale. He especially abhorred questions of the "Are Orcs Nazis or communists?" kind. Tolkien's purpose was both more specific and more universal.

"APPLICABILITY" VERSUS "ALLEGORY"

In *The Lord of the Rings*, Tolkien gives us an adventure in the form of a ring quest with a simple human moral truth at its centre. However, the nature of that adventure and that moral position were undeniably "applicable" to the most dramatic conflicts of the 20th century.

Although Tolkien did not intend to mimic the events of his time, he did acknowledge when he began writing *The Lord of the Rings* in 1937 that something of the impending conflict with Nazi Germany was discernible in the dark atmosphere of its composition. Furthermore, as the bulk of the book was written through the dark years of World War II, there were

Opposite: Orcs

aspects of the real war that were inevitably comparable to his "War of the Ring".

It is interesting to note Tolkien's own comments on this in his wartime letters to his son, Christopher, who was stationed with the British forces in South Africa. He sent chapters in serial form to Christopher as he wrote them, along with personal letters with constant references to Hobbits, Orcs and Rings – as similes for individuals and issues relating to actual events in the conflict with Germany.

"Well, there you are: a hobbit among the Urukhai," Tolkien wrote. "Keep your hobbitry in heart and think that all stories feel like that when you are in them." However, this did not mean that real events in the war shaped Tolkien's invented war. His "War of the Ring" was about ideals, not political realities. It essentially revolved around a human moral crisis, which he perceived in the real war, but not just in the enemy.

In one letter to Christopher, Tolkien wrote: "We are attempting to conquer Sauron with the Ring. And we shall (it seems) succeed. But the penalty is, as you will know, to breed new Saurons, and slowly turn Men and Elves into Orcs. Not that in real life things are as clear-cut as in a story, and we started out with a great many Orcs on our side …"

Clearly, Tolkien's war had its own direction to follow, which had no parallels in the war with Germany. This is not to say that Tolkien was neutral in his view of Hitler and Nazi Germany – far from it.

In 1941 he wrote to another son, Michael, who was at the time an officer cadet at the Royal Military Academy at Sandhurst:

I have spent most of my life, since I was your age, studying Germanic matters (in the general sense that includes England and Scandinavia). There is a great deal more force (and truth) than ignorant people imagine in the "Germanic" ideal … Anyway, I have in this War a burning private grudge – which would probably make me a better soldier at 49 than I was at 22: against that ruddy little ignoramus Adolf Hitler. Ruining, perverting, misapplying, and making forever accursed that noble northern spirit, a supreme contribution to Europe, which I have ever loved, and tried to present in its true light. Nowhere, incidentally, was it nobler than in England, nor more early sanctified …

Indeed, one might even perceive that this "grudge" against Hitler might have had something to do with Tolkien's ambitions in writing a new version of the ring quest.

RECLAIMING THE RING

In the 19th century Richard Wagner recognized the absolute centrality of the ring quest in the vast mythological themes of European and especially Germanic peoples. He consciously seized upon the ring as a symbol of the German identity, heritage and state. In the 20th century the music of Wagner's *The Ring of the Nibelung* became so closely allied with the Nazi Party and the rise of the Third Reich that they became synonymous in the popular mind. During World War II, the grand themes and traditions of the ring quest were usurped (or, as Tolkien saw it, ruined, perverted and misapplied) by the German state with which Tolkien's nation was at war.

On one level, *The Lord of the Rings* is certainly an attempt by Tolkien to reclaim the ring as a symbol of "that noble

northern spirit" which had fallen into such disrepute in
Germany. With some justification, Tolkien blamed Wagner
and his heirs for the dimming of the "true light". Although
Wagner's genius was indisputable, his politics were repugnant.
The great musician's family and heirs were not innocent dupes
of the Nazi Party. Wagner's ideological stance may to some
degree be evaluated by the fact that he chose to dedicate his
collected works to Arthur de Gobineau, the father of Aryan
racialist theory – a theory that Tolkien correctly rejected as
being as intellectually ridiculous as it was morally repellent.

To Tolkien's credit, he saw from the beginning the nature
of the Nazi obsession with Wagner's Ring Cycle. Perhaps
what appealed to the Nazis in the ring quest was an
idealization of the pursuit of power for its own sake. Tolkien
appreciated the ring quest tradition on many levels, but
having already lived through one world war, he understood
the nature of the curse of the "ring of power" as well as any
man could. He believed that even for the good man the
pursuit of power was in itself an evil that would enslave the
human spirit and soul. And, in the Third Reich, there were
not many "good men" to start with.

There can be little doubt that part of Tolkien's deeply
felt motivation in writing *The Lord of the Rings* was a desire
to set the record straight by reclaiming the ring quest
tradition, and presenting the "noble northern spirit" of
Europe in its "true light". Just as Tolkien chose on minor
points to "challenge" Shakespeare's use of myth and history
in *Macbeth*, on a much grander scale he "challenged"
Wagner's use of myth and history in his ring cycle operas
by writing *The Lord of the Rings*.

Opposite: Travellers on the High Pass through the
Misty Mountains

Tolkien understood the deep moral crisis at the centre of the ring quest as Wagner perceived it. He saw the devastation that the Iron Age mentality of the ring quest had wreaked in the world, and chose to reshape the ring quest fundamentally for the 20th century. He did this by turning the quest on its head. The ring of power was "unmade" by reversing the spell. The hero of the quest does not seize the ring but destroys it by dropping it into the inferno where it was made.

In 1937 Tolkien began to forge his "One Ring" imaginatively as a symbol for an absolute power that morally and physically contaminated all who touched it. He could not even have guessed how soon history would catch up with his dark vision and make his tale appear almost prophetic. He certainly could not have imagined how the scientists of the real world would soon create something that was every bit as powerful, evil and contaminating as the "One Ring" of Sauron the Dark Lord.

THE ONE RING AND THE BOMB

Although *The Lord of the Rings* was largely written during the war years, it was not published until 1954, and by this time the atomic bomb had seized the popular imagination. The public was less likely to equate Sauron with Hitler than the One Ring with the Bomb. It was difficult for many to believe that the idea of the One Ring was not inspired by the Bomb. Surely, some suggested, no place could look more like a nuclear testing ground than the ash-laden land of Mordor? There is no doubt that Tolkien was very much against the atomic bomb. On August 9, 1945, he wrote to Christopher: "The news today about 'atomic bombs' is so horrifying one is stunned. The utter folly of these lunatic physicists to consent to do such work for war purposes: calmly plotting the destruction of the world!"

Still, Tolkien was at pains to point out that the One Ring was fully formed long before he had any idea of the activities of atomic scientists. In a letter written in 1956, he found it necessary to state: "Of course my story is not an allegory of atomic power, but of Power (exerted for Domination)." However, he had to acknowledge that in a larger sense the message or moral of his novel certainly did not exclude atomic power. Indeed, Tolkien's views on nuclear weapons would not have been at all out of place at any Campaign for Nuclear Disarmament or Ban the Bomb meeting or protest march:

> Nuclear physics can be used for that purpose [bombs].
> But they need not be. They need not be used at all. If
> there is any contemporary reference in my story at all it
> is to what seems to me the most widespread assumption
> of our time: that if a thing can be done, it must be done.
> This seems to me wholly false. The greatest examples of
> the action of the spirit and of reason are in abnegation.
> When you say atomic power is "here to stay" you remind
> me that Chesterton said that whenever he heard that, he
> knew that whatever it referred to would soon be replaced,
> and thought pitifully shabby and old-fashioned. So-called
> "atomic" power is rather bigger than anything he was
> thinking of (I have heard it of trams, gaslight, steam-
> trains). But it surely is clear that there will have to be some
> "abnegation" in its use, a deliberate refusal to do some of
> the things it is possible to do with it, or nothing will stay!

A COUNTER-CULTURAL HERO?

Even retrospectively, however, it still seems very unlikely that such a self-confessed "old fogey" of an Anglo-Saxon professor, writing about a remote imaginary world filled with an impossibly obscure invented mythology, could suddenly find a huge American campus cult following in the midst of the radical, politically charged 1960s. Tolkien was nobody's idea of a radical campus professor, so what was it in his writing that was suddenly so relevant to the lives and politics of the youth culture of the 1960s, catapulting him into the category of one of the most popular authors of the century?

The answer was that Tolkien's approach to the ancient grand theme of the ring quest was as unconventional and inventive as his unlikely heroes, the Hobbits. In fact, *The Lord of the Rings* proved to be the perfect student counter-culture book. It was full of action and adventure, but it appeared ultimately to hold an anti-establishment, pacifist message. Frodo Baggins might not have been exactly a Hobbit Gandhi, but he did reject the temptations of worldly power to an almost saintly degree. The student anti-war and Ban the Bomb movements of the 1960s found an empathetic anti-hero in the Hobbit's humble values, as did the back-to-the-land hippie dropout culture. Tolkien could not have touched more bases with the youth culture of the 1960s if he had commissioned a market survey.

If Tolkien was ambiguous about the "meaning" of his tale, there is no doubt that the parallels between the One Ring and the Bomb were not missed by activists in the late 1960s and early 1970s. One need only read Robert Hunter's *The Greenpeace Chronicles* to see how closely allied the counter-culture was with Tolkien's world.

Greenpeace came into being in 1969 in Vancouver, Canada, as an ecological guerrilla organization that attempted to stop American nuclear testing on Amchitka Island in Alaska. To this end, it chartered its first ship and attempted to prevent the bomb from being exploded by sailing into the test area.

Writing about this maiden Greenpeace voyage, Hunter tells how they had arrived at a point where even the stout hearts of his shipmates saw their task as rather comically hopeless. "There was something superbly comical about it: here we were, eight green-clad amateur seamen, on our way to confront the deadliest fire of the age, like Hobbits bearing the ring toward the volcano of Mordor."

It was a comparison that carried them a long way. Like exhausted Hobbits, they persevered. If Hobbits could overcome the forces of Sauron, why couldn't a ragtag band of hippies overthrow the US military-industrial complex? At one point the valves and pistons of the old engine of their rather battered vessel required such coaxing and constant care on their long voyage along the north Pacific coast that the activists dubbed themselves the "Fellowship of the Piston Rings".

In Tolkien's tale, when the One Ring is finally destroyed, the subsequent volcanic eruption closely resembles a nuclear

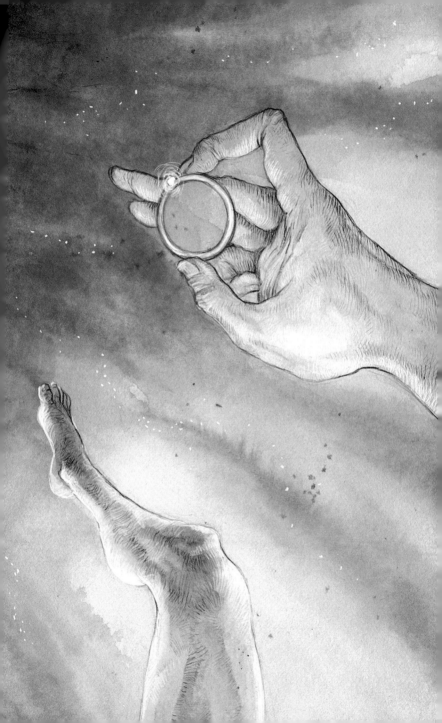

explosion – but an explosion that destroys only the evil forces of the Ring Lord. One might also see in that explosive "unmaking" of the One Ring the reversal of the traditional ring quest in a moral sense as well. That Iron Age mentality of "might equals right", which made the ring quest for power so important, ends with the nuclear age – when possession of such power entails only mutual destruction.

It was Albert Einstein who warned the world: "The unleashing power of the atom has changed everything except our way of thinking … we need an essentially new way of thinking if mankind is to survive."

NEW TIMES, NEW HEROES

Tolkien's reversal of the ring quest demonstrates this "new way of thinking". Its version of the quest represents a desire to change power structures. Tolkien saw the results of the pursuit of pure power in two wars, and rejected it. In his private mythic world he understood a human truth that modern technology has brought home to humankind with a terrible vengeance in the form of the nuclear bomb. If ever there was a manifestation of the ultimate power of the One Ring, the Bomb was it. The "Cold War" was the result of the grudging admission that power of the kind represented by nuclear weapons was ultimately self-destructive.

Tolkien also displayed this "new way of thinking" in his inspired choice of heroes. One must not forget the importance of his Hobbits; it would do no good to change the nature of the quest without changing the nature of the hero. Not only did Tolkien turn the ring quest on its head; he also reversed many of the characteristics usually expected of the quest hero.

Previous Page: Gollum's fall into the Fires of Doom

He wrote:

> The Hobbits are, of course, really meant to be a branch
> of the specifically human race (not Elves or Dwarves) …
> They are entirely without non-human powers, but are
> represented as being more in touch with "nature", and
> abnormally, for humans, free from ambition or greed of
> wealth. They are made small partly to exhibit the pettiness
> of man, plain unimaginative parochial man … and mostly
> to show up, in creatures of very small physical power, the
> amazing and unexpected heroism of ordinary men "at a
> pinch".

Ultimately, the greatest strength of Tolkien's Hobbits in their
epic struggle against all odds is their basic human decency.
It is their essential humanity, their simple but pure human
spirits, that allowed them to triumph in the end. And it is this
human element, combined with the grandeur and pomp of a
magnificently conceived mythic world, that has been the key
to Tolkien's continued popularity.

Characteristically, then, Frodo Baggins fails to live up
to the classic "hero" image at the time of the ultimate test.
At the last moment, on the edge of the Crack of Doom, the
Hobbit's resolve fails and he refuses to destroy the One Ring.
Virtuous though Frodo is, it is not the strength of his will that
allows the One Ring to be destroyed and Middle-earth to be
saved. It is Frodo's unprovoked and almost foolish charity
toward an undeserving enemy. Out of a sense of mercy,
the Hobbit allows the treacherous Gollum to live. Reason
should tell Frodo that Gollum will betray him again, but the
Hobbit chooses to obey his heart. In the end, the One Ring is
destroyed exactly because Frodo takes pity on his enemy, and

Gollum survives long enough to betray him again. On the edge of the Crack of Doom, Gollum wrestles with the Hobbit. Finally, he overcomes the weakened Frodo. He viciously bites off the Hobbit's ring finger. Then, seizing the One Ring, Gollum topples backward into the fiery abyss. The One Ring is destroyed.

In Frodo the Hobbit, Tolkien found a 20th-century Everyman who has, and will continue to have, universal appeal to people of any time and any place. In Tolkien's *The Lord of the Rings* the Hobbit teaches us that "attempting to conquer Sauron with the ring" is no longer the goal of the quest. In the end, it is not the power of the mind nor the strength of the body but the instincts of the human heart that save the world. It is the simple human capacity for mercy that finally allows evil to be overthrown.

Opposite: Frodo the Hobbit.
Next page: The Gates of Valhalla

INDEX

PAGE NUMBERS IN ITALIC TYPE REFER
TO ILLUSTRATIONS AND CAPTIONS

PAGE NUMBERS IN BOLD REFER TO CHARTS